STORIES OF HURT, HEALING & EVERYTHING IN BETWEEN



# WHEN WE FORGIVE

A LIFE TO PAPER ANTHOLOGY

Life to Paper Publishing
Toronto, ON Canada | Miami, FL U.S.A.
www.lifetopaper.com



For information about special sales, bulk purchases, speaking engagements, or author events, please contact Life to Paper Publishing at info@lifetopaper.com or visit www.lifetopaper.com.

10 9 8 7 6 5 4 3 2 1

Library of Congress Control Number: 2026906782

ISBN 978-1-997929-02-4; 978-1-997929-04-8 (paperback)
ISBN 978-1-997929-03-1 (hardcover)
ISBN 978-1-997929-05-5; 978-1-997929-06-2 (eBook)
ISBN 978-1-997929-07-9 (paperback, French flaps edition)

Cataloguing in Publication Data (CIP)
When We Forgive : stories of hurt, healing & everything in between / Life to Paper Publishing.
Includes contributions from fifteen authors.
ISBN 978-1-997929-02-4 (paperback) | ISBN 978-1-997929-03-1 (hardcover) | ISBN 978-1-997929-05-5 (eBook)

1. Forgiveness—Case studies. 2. Self-acceptance—Case studies. 3. Healing—Psychological aspects. 4. Mental health—Personal narratives. 5. Substance abuse—Recovery—Personal narratives.

*This collection exists because a community of storytellers chose to give their voices in service of others.*

*We carry what was done*
*and what we have done.*
*Somewhere between the two,*
*we begin to loosen our grip.*

# A NOTE ABOUT THIS COLLECTION

This anthology contains true stories shared by individual contributors reflecting on experiences of hurt, healing, forgiveness, and personal growth. Certain names, identifying details, and chronological sequences have been changed or combined to protect the privacy of individuals. Some contributors reference experiences connected to recovery communities or twelve-step programs. In keeping with the long-standing tradition of personal anonymity in such spaces, identifying details have been respectfully limited.

This publication is not affiliated with, endorsed by, or representative of Alcoholics Anonymous or any other twelve-step fellowship. The views and experiences shared are those of the individual contributors alone.

The stories and perspectives shared in this book do not represent professional, medical, psychological, or therapeutic advice. Readers should consult qualified professionals regarding any medical or mental-health concerns. Any resemblance to persons or events not explicitly described is coincidental.

Each contributor retains full ownership of their personal

story. Stories included in this anthology are published with permission of their authors. Publication in this collection does not restrict contributors from publishing or sharing their stories elsewhere in future works.

All contributors, editors, designers, and collaborators—including photographer Simon Tanenbaum (www.simontanenbaum.com)—have generously donated their time, talent, and creative work in support of this project.

All proceeds from the sale of this book support the Life to Paper Foundation, which helps individuals affected by mental health and addiction experience the therapeutic power of putting life to paper through books, writing workshops, and publishing scholarships.

# STORIES & VOICES

# A NOTE FROM THE EDITOR

I have wondered this: Who was the first to practice the act of forgiveness? What occasioned it? A small matter or a large one? A personal public slight or a dire offence?

What was the forgiver's calculus? How could the forgiver know what the act could accomplish? That something might be resolved. That healing might take place. That faith might be restored. Or that nothing might happen. The wound could not be sutured. The fracture could not be bound. The brokenness forever a silent, corrosive life companion.

The stories in this volume are explorations of the self, set upon by a breadth and depth of circumstances that are undeserved at best and violent at their worst, especially when youth and innocence are afflicted. These are stories of survival—questioning, penetrating, and searing. They open a window on why and how forgiveness matters.

The authors of these stories are generously donating the proceeds to the nonprofit arm of Life to Paper Publishing to support writers and mental health initiatives in accordance with Life to Paper's mission and goals, which can be found at lifetopaper.com. I am profoundly grateful for being able to play a small role as the editor of these stories—such a minute exchange for the wisdom I have been taught about our humanity in all its frailties and adversities—and capacity to endure.

*Don Loney*
*Toronto, ON*

# BROTHER JOHN

## NORM TRAINOR

Freud said the reason two siblings have a different perspective on their family of origin is that one-third of what we remember about our childhood happened, one-third is what other people described, and one-third is our representation of what happened.

I had a brother, John, who was fourteen months younger. Born in Northern Ireland, we were "Irish Twins." Growing up, we were inseparable. Yet, in an adult conversation with my brother, he commented that one of us had to be adopted because we were so different.

I was the classic first born—responsible, rule bound, and more cautious. John was impulsive and a free spirit who was constantly trying new things. He was a risk-taker from an early age.

My brother was also a gifted athlete with a Mensa IQ.

The trajectory of our lives is shaped by nature and nurture. There is an ongoing debate about whether successful people are born or made. In other words, do inherent traits determine success or failure, or is it nurturing that fosters our growth and wellbeing?

Our parents can be the most important influence in the nurturing we receive growing up. We assume that children in the same family will be parented in the same way. However, experience teaches us otherwise.

Birth order plays a role. So, too, does the dynamic between a child and a parent.

The following is the perspective I have of growing up, and its impact on John and me.

Throughout my life, my dad considered himself a failure. Prior to getting married and having children, he had been an excellent athlete and police officer in Northern Ireland who had been shot three times in a gun battle with an IRA leader. He almost died and, I suspect, suffered post-traumatic stress syndrome. As a result, he left the police force. Unfortunately, he never settled into a career. He married my mother and had two sons within the next three years. Both of my parents were very unhappy in the relationship. My dad struggled to define himself and increasingly sought solace in alcohol.

From my earliest recollection, he talked about his life retrospectively. It was as if his opportunity to build a successful life and career had been taken away. He was a wonderful salesman and a very charming man. Yet, he drifted from one job to another. He seemed unable to resolve his sense of loss and focus on a future direction that inspired him.

As a father, my dad encouraged me to excel in whatever I was doing, whether in academics or in sports. He used positive reinforcement.

With my brother, his critical parenting side came out. He saw himself in John. As a result, he was hard on John. Their relationship became fraught with tension.

John was in the top one percent of the population intellectually. Yet, he struggled in school. Where he excelled was in sports.

John did not learn to skate until he was ten. By the age of thirteen, he was an excellent hockey player with a natural and smooth stride. He was also big for his age and aggressive, and he played a tough, fast game. However, Dad became increasingly frustrated with John's struggles in school and forbade him to play hockey.

In high school, football became John's sport of choice. He matured early and was 6-foot-2, and 215 pounds at age fifteen. His natural athletic ability, combined with his size and aggressive nature, enabled him to excel on the football field. He earned a scholarship to a U.S. college. The coaching and discipline at the NCAA level in the U.S. nurtured his natural talents. He became a superb offensive lineman.

John came back to Canada and signed with the Toronto Argonauts. He became a starter as an offensive guard. He was 6-foot-3 and 245 pounds. His coaching in the U.S. enhanced his technical proficiency. His natural ability and aggressiveness combined with good coaching enabled him to excel as a professional athlete. He was so good, his coach hailed him as the best offensive lineman he had ever coached.

However, towards the end of his first season with the Argos, he sustained a serious knee injury. He came back the next year and played professionally for a few years. The knee injury, and other injuries, took its toll on him and impacted his performance over time. When he retired from football, he, too, struggled to define a career that he considered rewarding. As a result, he also struggled financially.

One of John's gifts was special intelligence. He was good with his hands; he worked as a grip on film sets. He loved the movie business, but it did not provide a steady income.

Shortly after retiring from professional football, John did not have enough money to cover his rent and monthly expenses. A pattern emerged, where when John struggled financially, he would turn to me for financial support. He was a proud man, and I am sure his sense of vulnerability at those times took its toll. In this particular instance, he knew my wife and I were doing some home renovations. He called me to ask for money to pay his rent and cover his expenses for the next month. We agreed that I would give him the required amount to cover his expenses in advance and he would start working with me that weekend. While I do not have John's spatial intelligence, I have a strong back and like to work quickly. I would provide labour support.

It was a long weekend coming up. We agreed that we could get a lot of the renovations done in three days. It would not interfere with my work and would give us some time together.

That weekend, John did not show up. A friend invited him to his cottage for the weekend. John did not even call to let me know. When he returned, he came to see me. I was doing what work I could in the basement to get a start on the renovation. John came downstairs and acted as if nothing had happened. I was enraged. The air turned blue as I vented my frustration. The basement windows were open on a hot July day. Our neighbours must have wondered what was going on.

We came close to blows. That was not the first time, nor the last time our disagreements led to, or almost led to, physical confrontation. One of the consistent themes in our relationship was that John seemed unable to apologize for an indiscretion or action that caused hurt feelings.

Throughout life, we encounter adversity. Often, we attribute feelings and emotions to activating events. But it is not the events in our lives that cause us to feel or respond in a certain way, it is our *beliefs* about those events. How we choose to interpret the events in our lives is what is most important.

Encountering adversity either makes us better or bitter. As John aged and became increasingly frustrated with his situation in life, he became more bitter.

Those who have good mental health live life to the fullest. Those who do not feel good about themselves or their circumstances wield their disappointment as a weapon of anger against those around them. Often, these are the people closest to them.

John had an ambivalent relationship with our father. Our dad lived to be ninety-two. For the last period of his life, he was dependent. He lived close to us. I would check in with him regularly. We provided financial support and care to ensure he was comfortable. He was, for me, a lovable man. However, he was not easy to care for.

One time, my family was on a two-week ski trip. I asked my brother to check in with Dad while we were away. When we returned, I went to see my dad. My brother showed up while I was making breakfast for Dad.

John was on edge. We left Dad's apartment together. Outside the building, John vented his frustration. He accused me of being away and leaving him to do the heavy lifting in looking after Dad. He said, "I want to beat the shit out of you."

On the ski trip, I had torn my ACL in my right knee. I said, "I am standing on one leg. That will make it a fair fight. Let's have it out right now." This was another instance of almost coming to blows. Over time, the tensions in our relationship led to us drifting apart.

I missed him. Pride and grievance on both sides pushed us apart.

Then, on a day burned in my memory, I received a call from John's wonderful life partner, Rita. John had been diagnosed with terminal cancer. I immediately went to see him. He was bedridden. I began to feel an enormous sense of loss and regret that I had let the tensions in our relationship push us apart.

John lived a few more months. We became as close as we had ever been. We talked candidly about our lives. It was a time of healing for both of us.

John did not apologize or express regret for the actions that I experienced as hurtful. It did not matter. He was my "Irish Twin" and I loved him deeply. I appreciated all the good things that he contributed to my life.

John died on December 21, 2017. At his Celebration of Life, hundreds attended to show their respect and affection for John. He touched many lives. Like our dad, he had the gift of seeing greatness in others and not in himself.

When I think about him now, as I often do, it is in remembering the good times, the love we shared, and our bond as brothers.

Norm Trainor is the president of The Covenant Group Toronto, Canada, specializing in sales force effectiveness, business and practice management, and customized learning programs.

# NOTES TO MY MOTHER

VERA TARMAN

Books were my friends. I read the same stories repeatedly—favourites that kept me company during long evenings alone in my room. When my mother died, I was halfway through *The Outsiders*. Johnny and Ponyboy's story had me in tears. I folded my grief for my mother into their world, between their rumbles and street fights, and especially into that "Stay Gold" prayer. My mother was gold, too, and, like Johnny, she was gone. The hurt and upset of being left behind had nowhere else to go.

Sometimes I wrote in my journal, but the words burned hot with emotion. I had to stop writing, shoving the pages under my pillow. My thoughts about her seemed to come in violent clusters and then turned into bullies that shoved me around, needling me with hot insults.

Her last words had come through a phone call. "You know, I love you," she had said, her voice low, barely perceptible.

That memory haunted me. I had sighed heavily into the receiver. She was back on the tenth floor of the psychiatric hospital, on the ward that required a special elevator, the one you had to buzz to access. My father had told me she was on suicide watch again and couldn't leave the floor unattended.

He doesn't want her coming home, I thought, standing in our empty kitchen. He's had enough of her screaming and her threats that she'd kill him. And her falling in the hallway on her visits to the bathroom. Sometimes, she would lie on the floor all night.

I knew it was just the whiskey, but I was tired of it, too.

I waited, hearing her breathing on the phone, wondering if she was waiting. I hoped she wouldn't ask me to visit. If she wanted cigarettes, she might want me to come over to take her outside. But I hated the streetcar ride downtown in the night. And the hospital was all wrong; there were so many hallways with locked doors, and nurses rushing past with their heads down. Her tiny room was depressing, too. It was small enough to hold only a bed, with an end table pushed to the wall and two lacquered ashtrays she'd made in occupational therapy. She had floor-to-ceiling windows that overlooked College Street, but they were made of thick glass and impossible to open. Every time I visited, I would check. No way to open them for even a slight breeze. Only the washrooms had bright light, and I wondered, looking up at the ceiling, if someone was watching her in there, making sure washing was all she was doing.

She had nothing more to say. I mumbled goodbye and hung up the phone. I did not know it would be the last time we would speak.

Three days later, I was sitting in my aunt's garden. She wasn't really an aunt, but a family friend who invited me over whenever my mother was in the hospital. We'd just heard that my mother had escaped from the locked ward. They didn't explain how; maybe she slipped in the elevator pretending she was a nurse on the ward—she actually *was* a nurse. We were waiting for news while I played absently with the dog. It was very tense.

The call came that afternoon. My aunt walked into the summer heat where I was still sitting with the dog. I did not want to hear what she had to say, but I did not know how to stop her. I stood up.

"They found her," she said. "Grenadier Park. Dead in the pond, with a bottle of Five Star whisky on the shore."

High Park. We lived in the neighbouring Roncesvalles. She must have used her last cigarette money to get there. Guess she wanted to die close to home. Or where my father played chess with the other German men on weekends. Did she think of him as she drank on the shore, contemplating her next moves? I wondered what my mother looked like when they found her.

I turned away, as if looking for an escape. Was this bad news? Should I cry? It felt like relief. Confusion washed over me, followed by a dark heaviness in my chest, like pain, like one of the schoolyard bullies sitting on my sternum. Maybe I could ignore it. Could I eat enough cookies or hide upstairs in the bedroom with my book, or maybe walk the dog deep into the ravine where no one could find us? He loved to walk with me.

I felt guilty for feeling relief that she was finally dead. After three years of suicide attempts, police visits, neighbours pounding on walls, I was exhausted. I was only fourteen. And I was furious. She'd said she loved me, but her kind of love meant broken promises and disappointments. It meant pathetic attempts to make me dinner or to get up for work in the morning. She usually ended up being sent home before noon.

Years later, I read that suicide survivors typically felt guilty. They feel that should have done more to save their loved ones. I felt that, but mostly I felt relief that it was over. I had done enough, so mainly I felt anger and relief; the sadness came later. But at that time, those feelings brought their own terror: I was certain my mother would return in the darkness of night to collect me and drag me into her world as punishment for feeling nothing but relief that she died.

That made me too afraid to attend her funeral. When I heard it was sparsely attended, I guessed she'd be hurt and mad about this. I should have been there. She had only a few friends left; she had worn down most of the others with her late-night calls, full of crying and promises that never held up.

"She'll never forgive me," I told my therapist years later.

"Maybe," she said, "it's really you who needs to forgive your mother." I couldn't see that. I should have felt sad. She would be mad that I was glad she was dead.

My mother had been excellent at apologies. I had learned to tune them out, even hate them, and hate *her* when she said them. What good were sorry words when the same thing happened the next day? Well, now it was finished.

I avoid washing my hair as much as possible because she had died in water. I knew she'd come back for me when I was in the shower, defenceless and naked. I would whimper under the shower nozzle, convinced I could see her shadow looming, waiting in the bathroom corner. A black presence ready to pounce, to thrust my head underwater and take me with her.

Librarians became my first therapists. During those early years, I devoured stories of abandoned children, adult children of alcoholics, memoirs of people destroyed by drink. I was fascinated by the destructive urge that drove human beings toward darkness, especially of the alcoholic variety. Librarians helped me find these books. I called it "bibliotherapy." It was a new term that helped me process pain through other people's words.

After her death, I'd promised myself never to drink. That unsubstantial resolve melted with my first drink. I felt the fuzzy warmth that blurred the anger that had become a hard rock lodged beneath my ribs. All those books helped me understand my mother's disease, but I still felt the rawness that quickly became fury or scalding tears whenever I mentioned her to therapists. So, I rarely talked about her, focusing instead on the consequences of my anger. How to recognize the triggers; how to mop up the damage of an outburst. The booze didn't soothe my pain, but it muffled it in a pillow-like funnel where I could blast my rage outward.

My anger got worse the more I drank. I was immune to its fire now, but it cost me jobs, friends, living arrangements, low grades.

"You're a mean drunk," I told myself, looking in the mirror one day. I didn't want to be mean, so I quit drinking, and the anger rumbled underneath, erupting every few months into a shouting match, or a threatening push of a friend, or inappropriate words at work. Sometimes I scared myself.

I was forty when I picked up my first spiritual book. Until then, I'd consumed psychology, biology, psychiatry—anything that explained why people did the awful things they did. I had studied to become a physician, focusing on treating substance abuse and addictions. I found comfort in murder mysteries and thrillers, thinking I had compassion for the darker side of human nature, and could even thrive in it. We all carried darkness. I certainly did.

One sweltering afternoon on a trip to Thailand, I sat in a bookstore cafe, hot and exhausted. My hand found Eckhart Tolle's book on the shelf. I had walked past his work for years, dismissing it. But that day, something shifted. I felt compelled to open it.

Then came *A Course in Miracles*. The writing was dense, circular, maddeningly impenetrable. But its message was clear and relentless: forgive, only forgive. It sounded simple, but the book offered no instructions. "But how?" I muttered to myself, flipping pages. "Exactly who do I forgive? What do I do?" I would throw the book down in frustration. I knew its message was important, but how to make it happen?

The book offered no roadmap, just the relentless repetition of that single message.

Around this time, I had also started attending AA meetings. I had quit regular drinking years earlier, but I kept returning to it, convinced I could manage one or two glasses of wine each night. It never worked out that way. I always ended up having too many drinks and then binging on sweet carb-laden foods until I felt sick to my stomach. It disgusted me, yet I could not stop.

The rooms surprised me. There were friendly voices, and I heard unexpectedly uplifting stories. I had been to a few meetings in the past for friends who were celebrating their one-year medallions. The medallion holders were always so pleased with themselves, which I admittedly found bizarre. I had made sobriety for a year several times. What was the big deal? Well, to each their own. I had resolved and kept away from what seemed like pretend happiness.

But this time, I was compelled to visit the inner sanctums of the closed meetings where people would speak of the intimate details of their lives. It was strange, sharing so much without the obligations of actual friendship, no strings attached. It was exactly what I needed.

But I was puzzled: These were people I would never have approached otherwise. I had tried finding similar connections like these in churches, joining various committees, or voluntary or political groups, but those conversations felt hollow compared to this raw honesty.

The women's meetings especially drew me in. They talked about husbands who disappointed them, jobs that drained them, and children who worried them. They mentioned a fourth step, an eighth step, a ninth step.

"What are those?" I asked one woman after a meeting.

She smiled. "The steps are where we look at our resentments and make amends. Where we learn to let go of our baggage. Where we learn to forgive."

I thought of that circular book, *Course in Miracles*, and its impossible instructions—only forgive. Was here finally a way to understand the mechanics of forgiveness? The steps to how to actually forgive?

Then, one day, a woman talked about how she tried to apologize to her child. Her voice was trembling as she described kneeling in front of her daughter, looking into her child's eyes and promising to do better. She would stop drinking and make it right again. I felt something crack open inside me. Instead of glazing over, thinking, *I have heard this all before*, I cried. My tears were unexpected, so sudden and overwhelming. I wiped my face, embarrassed, but the ache was too old and deep to hide. I could not keep it back; I had to say something, finally. When the meeting ended, I found the woman outside the door, standing by the smoke butt can, her coat wrapped around her thin shoulders, holding a cigarette and a coffee.

"Can I talk to you?" I asked, my voice thick. She nodded, moving aside so we could have privacy near the bike rack, away from the shouts and laughter of others. I didn't bother with small talk. "Apologies mean nothing," I blurted, surprising even myself with the harshness of my words. "They mean nothing if you're still planning to go on killing yourself. Your child won't remember the apology. She'll remember the hurt, the way you keep choosing the drink over her. Words mean nothing." My voice broke, and I could hear myself choking with tears, but I couldn't stop. I was speaking to this woman, but really, I was speaking to my mother—to the angry ghost that still hovered every night that I slept alone, stone cold sober. "She will only remember how you left her, over and over. That's what stays." I gulped before I continued, worried that I might be hurting her feelings.

She listened. She didn't interrupt or flinch. She just nodded; she seemed to absorb every word I said. I kept talking, pouring out the things I never could say to my mother: the accusations, my fears of her coming back in the middle of the night, my desperate need to be seen by her, to be chosen by her. By the end of this outpouring, I was raw and felt exposed, but that woman had stayed with me, holding my gaze. In fact, a couple of other women had come over to our corner and listened closely. In that moment, I realized: this mother, not mine, heard me. She really heard me.

After the coffee break, we were back in the rooms; I sat on the edge of a battered metal chair. I felt emptied and strangely light. For years, I had clung to my grievance like a badge of honour. I was the motherless child, forgotten in the face of her addiction. I was convinced that my forgiveness could only come when I was ready to let go, and now I saw clearly how I had not been ready to let go. Why would I let go before someone out there knew I had suffered too? That I'd been hurt, neglected, left behind? I wanted my pain to be seen, to be acknowledged. I was just as important as my mother, who got all the attention in our house, and I deserved more than a meaningless apology.

I saw the woman nodding, understanding. It fit with something we say in AA: faith without works is dead. Words without action are just noise. This woman hadn't considered that before, she said after I was done. She'd always thought an apology was enough. But now she saw how empty words could become just another excuse, a way to avoid changing, maybe even relapse again. And she was going to act differently based on hearing me. She would change so that the apology would not be necessary.

I felt more unburdened than I ever had in any therapy session. I had told a *mother* my perspective. I had spoken my truth I'd carried for so long. And in doing so, I felt the terrible anger within me start to melt. I felt ready to let go, ready to forgive my mother. I was sure she had forgiven me for not going to her funeral, for being glad that part of our life was over. It was time for me to forgive.

In the weeks that followed, I kept coming back to those meetings. I could listen to the women in a new way. I heard their pain, not just my own. I learned to feel the pain of the mothers, their anguish over their child, and I knew my mother must have felt that same anguish. I even felt hope that some might find sobriety and give their children a new life. Each time a woman with children announced another day sober, I felt a surge of gratitude. I thanked her, and said, "You are my mother spirit." Sometimes I saw the surprise in her eyes, sometimes tears.

I knew my own mother hadn't gotten sober, but someone else's mother had, and that was enough. There was a kind of universal mother in those rooms, a spirit that made sure I was not forgotten. If it happened for one child, it happened for the child within me. Call it vicarious forgiveness. Call it a higher power's order of forgiveness.

It's 2 a.m., I'm standing in the park wearing pyjamas and my partner's housecoat, the fabric rough against my arms where the sleeves have bunched up. There is a small encampment nearby of four or five tents and garbage in mounds all over the park. Someone walks past the AIDS memorial with slow steps, their footsteps echoing off the concrete. My puppy is sniffing around a pile of bags, her nose digging in and out of them, her tail wagging in circles. She stays close enough that I can see the white patches on her fur faintly in the park light. I can't believe I'm doing this—standing here in the park, in the middle of the night, my feet cold in plastic flip-flops, just so she can pee. The air smells slightly damp from a rain that we had hours earlier. My eyes feel tired with sleep. Finally, she squats near a tent, her back legs trembling slightly. It's too dark to see clearly, but I can hear the soft stream of pee against a tarp.

I had always wanted a dog. It was one of those childhood promises that never materialized. "Your father won't like it," my mother had said, waving her hand while lighting a cigarette.

When I finally got my own place, I got a dog. It was in a small apartment in Windsor, in the back of a store that I worked in. A small one bedroom, it had thin walls and a carpet full of stains. I was chuffed; it was my place, with a kitchen and bathroom and living room. Micki was a yappy little puppy. Some kind of mutt with ears that stood up, always alert, always listening. I had no idea how to care for him. His first owner was thrilled that I could take this extra puppy from a litter and told me to just feed him and take him out.

I knew dogs needed food, so I filled a bowl twice a day, and watched him attack the kibble. But when I took him outside to pee, he just sniffed around the fence and fire hydrant, his nose working and working while I shifted from foot to foot, checking my watch. "Come on," I would mutter, tugging the leash. I'd get impatient and stomp back into my apartment. Predictably, he'd pee on the carpet within minutes. A yellow stain spread across the rug that was getting darker over the weeks. This happened day after day. I found this maddening, my jaw clenching each time I reached for paper towels, the ammonia smell burning my nostrils. Shouting at him to pee didn't work; he'd just look at me with those dark eyes, head tilted in confusion. What really got me was that he was also a noisy yapper, his sharp barks cutting through my day. What did he want? The sound literally gave me a headache. Eventually, I put him in the bathroom tub and shut the door. There, he could pee and bark while I pressed a pillow over my head until the noise stopped.

Neighbours complained. The older man from next door, his face tight with anger under his baseball cap, knocked on my door, his words pointed: "You should not have a dog." Another neighbour threatened to call animal control. I protested that the dog would not listen to me, but they turned away with disgust. At the end of that summer, I had to leave the apartment, and someone took the dog from me. I was embarrassed. I could see that I was ill-equipped to take care of the dog and swore I'd never have children —or another dog—again. The evidence was clear: I didn't know how to mother anything small and helpless. I was my mother's daughter, after all.

But here I was, forty years later, my breath forming small puffs in the cold air that dissipated as quickly as they appeared. I never had a child. But now I had this dog—a small designer puppy that I found advertised on the internet. This is my second attempt at mothering. I read the books this time, highlighting passages about schedules and being consistent; I even hired a dog trainer. I knew what to do: Every hour for every month of age, you take the dog out to pee. That meant setting alarms that would jolt me out of sleep, pulling myself out of bed. I would carry this puppy to the park next to our house, her warm body squirming against my chest. I would stand there until she peed, no matter how long it took. I was willing to inconvenience myself, to sacrifice my sleep, for her.

I had discovered something unexpected. Standing there shivering in my pyjamas and housecoat in the fall air, I hadn't expected to feel anything but tired and cold. My toes were numb in my flip-flops, the dampness of the previous rain seeping through. The park was quiet except for the distant hum of taxis and Ubers and noise in the nearby tents and the soft rustle of leaves. But when she squatted and peed in the park's dark, her tail wagging with accomplishment, something shifted in my chest. A warmth that had nothing to do with temperature.

Is this what a mother feels? *Did my mother feel this when I was small, before the alcohol?* The next thought came unbidden, sharp: I knew she did. Before the drinking got bad, before the promises turned sour. Maybe she'd stood in similar darkness, holding me, waiting for me to fall asleep, to stop crying, to just be okay. I bet she felt this same strange satisfaction mixed with exhaustion.

Is this why motherhood changes women? I knew this was just a dog, that real motherhood would offer problems I couldn't even imagine. But I had a taste of something I'd never experienced before—the peculiar satisfaction of showing up even when it was inconvenient, even when every cell in my body wanted to crawl back into bed—actually *wanting* to do it. What I gave to another—in this case, my puppy—somehow circled back to fill something empty in myself. *Love in action,* I thought, watching my puppy sniff around one more tree before we headed home, her tail still wagging, oblivious to the late hour. I had come to understand *forgiveness in action.*

Forgiveness changes, even matures. When my mother died, I'd tried to understand and make sense of it, relying on the forgiveness tenets of the Christian faith. But it wasn't enough; my fourteen-year-old self had stared at the crucifix, angry, and had written in my journal: "Damn you and your love; what good does your death do for me?" Years later, at her graveside, my thirty-year-old self wrote a poem to her, declaring that her death no longer caused me fear. "We have a new relationship now." As I stood in the cold graveyard, these words comforted me.

Now, close to seventy years of age, I realize the pain was still not over, because words are not enough.

Now I have more than words. I have the mothers in the AA rooms who listened when I needed to be heard, and some of whom even changed. I've changed, too, giving extra time to those who need it, the way I once needed it. I can hold those who suffer now and hope with those who dare to hope and try again.

Standing in that park at 2 a.m., watching my puppy squat in the damp grass, I understood something I couldn't have grasped at my mother's graveside: forgiveness isn't something I can achieve once and leave behind. It's something I need to practice, like all of us in those rooms who practice sobriety, one day at a time, one small act at a time.

Maybe that's enough. Maybe that's how it works. Not through perfect understanding, but through the quiet repetition of showing up, even when it's inconvenient, even when it's cold and dark and I'd rather be sleeping.

Dr. Vera Tarman is the medical director of one of Canada's largest treatment centres for substance abuse. She is a world-renowned food addiction expert, who writes, speaks, and treats people who suffer from food (sugar and flour) addiction. She is the author of *Food Junkies: Recovery from Food Addiction*, which is now in its second edition. She is also cohost of the popular *Food Junkies* Podcast, along with Molly Painschab and Clarissa Kennedy. You can also find her at her free Facebook group "I'm Sweet Enough: Sugar-Free for Life" and her YouTube channel @*Veratarmanmd*.

# SELF-FLAGELLATION

C.V. SHAW

---

> Mistakes are always forgivable, if one has the courage to admit them.
>
> BRUCE LEE

---

She wasn't an easy person. She wasn't! I remember.

And she was seldomly sweet, but when she was, it wasn't with me. With me, she was always angry. It was with strangers' kids, relatives, or my ex-husband. He had her heart. He once pinned me against the wall and she turned away, later to blame me.

It was personal. It was unfair. It was there. It was there where I detached. My fists loosened and I let her go, like when a spirit detaches and the body goes limp because there's nothing to hold onto anymore. The essence escaped. The fingers of betrayal ripping away at the tissues, destroying the nerve endings, gangrene rotting the connections—securing the wound could never cauterize. In that space and time, I lost my mother.

I know why she did it. *Love.* It was out of love. But I didn't understand her way of loving, and she didn't understand mine. I needed hugs, kisses, affection, and security. Lots and lots of security. I remember sleeping with my leg over hers, as if the weight of my skinny little leg would hold her in place. A place right close to me, touching. The heat emanating from between our legs would weld us; I would become one with her to make sure she could never separate from me while we slept—or ever! And while awake, I'd anchor my little figure onto hers, trying to melt into her, but most times, probably all times, my little body on her lap was a disturbance. *I* was a disturbance, and she'd quickly release me.

"You're making me too hot," she'd complain.

Didn't she realize that was the purpose? The heat would fuse us.

She didn't move me off her because she didn't love me—she did—but because she just wasn't the affectionate type. She was the type of person I envy. Those born under astrological earth signs. I wished to be one of those. Numb. Unaffectionate. Unfazed.

Back then, she didn't defend me from my ex, because she was defending my marriage, instead. Because she loved me so much that she didn't want me to end up like her—single, one income, no physical help, in all sense of the term, alone ... lonely. Lonely and judged! Judged by a society that saw divorce as a failure. Worse was spinsterhood. It meant there was something wrong with you, and therefore a reflection of those who raised you.

She tried with all her means to save my marriage, as she did with hers. Both failures. She finally divorced my father when I was seventeen. He had left her when she was pregnant with me. But she was relentless in saving a marriage that was dead, buried, and reincarnated into a marriage with another woman, while she was still hoping he'd come back to her. And she wanted me to be the same. To never give up.

She wanted me to not end up like her, while at the same time creating a carbon copy.

I never stopped loving her, but I did stop calling her "Mom." The mom factor had been shattered like float glass. I referred to her by "Cocho," short for Consuelo. It's what everybody called her. That heat that grew under my little leg, pretzeling hers, went cold. And, instead, resentment grew like the roots of a majestic Weeping Willow fissuring the soil of my being.

Looking back, I don't remember ever having called her "Mom." There was no well to fetch that memory from anymore. She could not remind me that once upon a time, I did call her "Mom." So, I began to call her "Mom" again when she was in a place between here and a galaxy far, far away. Even then, she was most likely hearing *her* mother's voice drowning out my own. I'll never know if she heard me call her "Mom" again, but I did. But does it count if she didn't hear me? Can I see her ears one more time, please. And not the grey ones under the mortician's bad makeup. Ones that are warm, alive, connected to her soul. Can I please just have *one more chance*?

I blamed her for everything that went sideways in my life. All caused by my low self-esteem, non-existent confidence, and an unawareness that self-love was a thing. I tried it her way. I put my ex-husband first, as she did with the illusion of my father. Then again with my second husband. I couldn't put myself first, because there was no *self* to put first. I was soft putty to be molded—no boundaries, just submission. Did it ever occur to her to think, *What about us? What about her? What about me?* Which place did we have or would we ever have?

We never found our place, like nomads forever trying to fit in a space that would hold us, but only temporarily, never finding our happily ever after ... not even with each other.

The animosity in me grew like wild fungi, as did her need to control my life. She wanted a second chance. She wanted a redo, and I was the carcass her broken dreams would possess. Regardless of being an adult. A single mother even, she'd made sure to drive me like a chess piece. She pushed me to get married at eighteen, instead of pushing me to go to college. And in my forties, as I yawned my way through university night classes, single, lonely, and with two kids at home, I cursed her. For every bump along the road—and there were many—I blamed her.

As she grew old, she softened. Out of resentment, I got harder, because my life was harder. When she offered a kind word or gesture, I barked. It was a habit built over many years of blocking her control antics. It was a knee-jerk reflex. There were times I wouldn't even open the door if she visited unexpectedly, even if it took her twenty minutes to get from her car to my front door. How I wish I could hand her a key today. Memories like these make me want to scrape my nails through my chest, extract my heart, and return it to God. Unworthy! Deserving of the flog!

I held her responsible for my mishaps and bad luck, but my biggest complaint is why she didn't tell me. Why didn't she make me understand that one day, I would not be able to forgive myself for being the daughter I was to her. There are worse ones out there, I'm sure, but that makes no difference to me nor her. Our relationship, our flawed connection, was mutually ours. Nobody else's. I was an extension of her—a divine cord constructed of cellular love. I could have tried to understand her choices by simply asking. I could have laughed at her dramatic outbursts. I could have hugged her while her body had life ... while I still had a mother.

I chose to punish her instead. Punish her for loving me in her way, and now, it's too late. There's no negotiating. There's no bargaining. There's only God darned guilt! Gut twisting, heart piercing guilt, subsequently followed by believing that she hears me when I blow words of self-pity into the empty space before me, begging her for forgiveness and directing them upwards to heaven, where I imagine she's finally found her place.

While I stay down here swimming in the karmic ocean of shame. The water's thick and heavy—like fresh cement spreading into my core, drying away rationed joy. My heart—dry, hard, and lifeless. The slab—burying a screaming child. A child—forever an irresponsible one, at that! It was my responsibility to save her. She gave me life, and I was supposed to do the same in exchange. So, why couldn't I save her? I'm in the medical field. I help people heal and feel better for a living. Why couldn't I do the same for her?

At a family gathering, she once complained of shoulder pain. She blamed her sleeping position on her tight sofa. She had a bed but slept on the couch to be able to hear if any intruders tried to break in since she lived alone. She was seventy-five percent deaf by old age. She couldn't hear a break-in if she tried, and she refused to wear a hearing aid. I think she watched way too many cop shows and probably had a defense plan in place. That was probably a bucket-list item for her—kick some motherfucker's ass!

I watched her show the family how she couldn't turn her shoulder in such a specific way. She was as dramatic as she had always been. She didn't sit on a chair and converse quietly about it; she stood and made the family her audience.

I looked up at her and said, "Well, sleep different, then!"

"How would you like me to sleep?" she asked, theatrically, with a space between words.

I lay on the couch and crossed my arms over my chest, corpse-like. "Like this," I said, then holding my breath.

My cousins laughed at my jest, and so did I. It *was* funny. But it's not now. It's not funny at all. It was mean! I could have helped her. But she was never satisfied with anything I did, which hardly made me want to do anything for her at all. Never good enough.

Could I have helped her as she lay on that hospital bed? Even with my medical background, I was incapable of making an intelligent medical decision when doctors asked—afraid it would be the wrong one.

The truth is, it was beyond what I could do, so I didn't try. I didn't even try. Instead, I gave up on her. I let her go. I let her go, again. This time *her* fists loosening. She was letting go of me too. In my heart, she was quietly saying, "You're not worthy of me staying tethered to this planet." But I know, beyond my wounds, she was saying, "I'm sorry. I'm sorry for moving your little body off mine. I'm sorry for not being sweet with you. I'm sorry for not defending you. I'm sorry for dying."

I should not have joked at that family gathering. I should have stayed silent; as silent as her last living second.

At that precise moment, all noises ceased, as if the ears, eyes, mouth, nose, and hands had disappeared. Her senses turned off as if by a grand and precise flick of a switch, and just like that, she became the vastness of non-existence. And so did I, in a sense, standing at her cold feet whispering, "I forgive you, Mom. Please forgive me."

The silence consumed me like the deep black ocean. And I wanted to be consumed, swallowed by the same invisibility that vacuumed her spirit. Because how dare I exist without her? Didn't we meld, even just a little? Enough that, if she went, so would I.

Instead, the divine detachment left a deep wound at the site of our physical connection. A gaping hole with stretched-out little hands reaching, trying to grab the air where she had left a trail of quickly dissipating, intangible essence. Draining. Dripping of longing and regret. Ulcerated by finitude.

I felt my heart breaking, little bits at a time. Millions of pieces throughout my body, shattered. Jagged shards clashing with each other, contrarily sounding like champagne glasses clinking with every shallow breath I took. The mental torment, like lashes on the skin of my back.

I had to accept that it was because she loved me so much that she wanted what she thought was best for me. But deep in my psyche, I also had to accept that, at the soul level, I loved her so much that I refused to have a long-lasting happy marriage. If she couldn't have it, neither would I. That wouldn't be fair to her. She'd always need someone to be by her side, and that would be me. If she went down single, we'd go down single together.

I understand now that I refused to accept anyone else's love if I couldn't have hers the way I wanted it—the way it should have been. I needed hers first. And then, I needed her forgiveness. It was the only way I would be able to begin to forgive myself. Sometimes, I imagine she decided to leave so that I wouldn't use her as an excuse anymore and, perhaps, let myself be loved. That was a phrase she'd say to me often—"Let yourself be loved." She'd ask why I wouldn't, but the awareness hit me like a bucket of cold water poured over me, only after she'd passed. I would not let myself be loved until she loved me the way I needed her to. In a Hallmark kind of way. I was sick of having to buy empty greeting cards, because the ones with writings shared words for a mother-daughter bond that we never had. And it angered me! It angered me that no one told me to fix things while I had a chance.

There was so much I felt ashamed of. The thought of redemption seemed impossible in this lifetime. Acts I could control like calling my absent father "Dad" the one or two times a year I saw him. Why in the world would I call him "Dad" and not her "Mom"? He was not deserving of it, but she wanted me to. I never asked her why, but I know she just wanted to make me feel like I did have a father.

But even for those circumstances where I had no control, I am still held hostage to her intimidation. I'm still afraid of making her angry. My granddaughter Abigail was born a year after Mom passed. I remember her requesting to the heavens, that all she wanted more than anything was to meet her great-grandkids. She didn't. But guess who did? Dad! Dad did. He met Abby just days before he had a stroke on the anniversary of Mom's passing. Like Mom, he spent three months suffering in a hospital bed before he passed. But he was on time to steal Mom's wish, and it riddled my every cell with guilt because it was I that invited him for Christmas. I was still in need of a parent figure. A sense of security, even if it was a false one. I needed it, and so I called, and he came—and, like the Grinch, nabbed her gift!

I have felt the pain of a hot stove-top on my palm, an iron, cigarette ashes on my knee, but nothing has ever physically burned more than the tears that scorch my eyes when I think about my mom missing out on the things she loved about life—just like me missing out on her.

I never thought I'd miss her. I always thought I'd be okay when she transitioned. I was so sure of it. Perhaps I was certain because I never actually thought about it. I don't think I'd allow those thoughts to submerge into my brain. If I didn't think of it, it wouldn't be. I was reversing René Descartes' philosophical point of, if you think it, it exists. I knew deep down inside, the pain would be unfathomable, and so my brain never created the possibility.

I miss her so much I fear God will take me to her because he thinks I prefer to be with her than without her, somehow launched through the sparkly constellations and into her majestic, enigmatic world—with no return ticket. I'm scared that I might just be okay with that.

See, I can't let her go and I can't get her back ...

So, I write. I write about her in poems, short stories, and long stories. I make up stories in my head. Like a magician, turning cards to coins, I recreate memories and hope they'll stick; like a defiant teenaged girl flinging wet globs of toilet paper onto the school bathroom ceiling.

I make up stories where I was patient and she was sweet. Stories where I remember calling her "Mom," and others where she'd kiss my cheek because I have no memory of her thin lips on my thirsty skin or her strong arms around my yearning body.

I write to acknowledge her. For my readers to know her. I want to show her off... "That's my mom!" I want to give her place to her—a place of honour.

I want to honour her!

I know she feels it, even if she is galaxies away. I know she sits with her head held high on a throne made for heavenly queens, accepting her new invisible body vibrating of dignity.

Now, I let her come to me. For three years, I didn't allow myself to feel her presence. I'd even force myself awake if I began to dream of her.

Blinded by shame, I couldn't see the hands of grief suffocating me were my own. And I think I'd prefer to die by self-murder than have to live without her forgiveness—which I needed in order to forgive myself.

But one day, I became brave, and I asked Dad why. What happened between them? Why did he do what he did to her—to us? He paused, glassy eyed, and looked down. His voice cracking, he said, "I was young. We were young ..."

I interrupted him. "It's okay, it's okay," I said, patting his thigh and trying to hide a teetering tear from falling out of my eye. Right there and then, an awareness of love draped over me, and I understood so much. I felt her pain of being abandoned while pregnant. I felt his pain of feeling trapped by a new love. I felt God's love birthing me to life through them: flawed, imperfect, trying, fulfilling their purpose as a human—just like me. And in this rapture of an epiphany, I forgave him. Mom forgave me, and I forgave myself.

I felt her hands, like a tingly soft wave, take away the gritty knotted rope from mine.

"I love you, Mommy," I told her, laying on my side, face to face on my bed.

"I'm so glad to hear you say that," she said, as her image faded into the skin behind my eyelids.

---

> "Guilt is the source of sorrows; 'tis the fiend, the avenging fiend that follows us behind with whips and stings."
>
> SHAKESPEARE, *MACBETH*

---

C.V. Shaw is a doctor of Oriental Medicine and a MindScape Instructor residing in Miami. Her publishing history includes contributing to magazines and newspapers, journal- and anthology-published poetry, and short stories. Her award-winning debut novel *The Spell* was published in 2020. Her short story *Ripped,* which was adapted to a short film *Channel 0*, earned seven film festival laurels including Madrid Int'l Film Festival. Shaw is also a board member for South Florida Writers Association.

# FREE AS I NEED TO BE

TABITHA ROSE

*Forgiveness.* With my father—it's complicated.

For a long time, I used to say I was a mistake. That was the language I carried as a child, and words matter more than we realize.

My parents were in love in the way young people often are—intensely, imperfectly, without a clear map for what comes next. And then I came along. Not long after, their relationship unraveled.

From the age of five until I was fourteen years old, I didn't see my father. Nine years is a long time in a child's life. Long enough to forget the sound of someone's voice. Long enough for a face to blur at the edges. Long enough for a person to become more story than memory.

I never tried to not hold him in my memory. It was quieter than that. More like he slowly faded into the background of our lives. We didn't talk about him much in our house; his name didn't float easily through the rooms.

Children are perceptive in ways adults often underestimate. I learned there were certain moments when it was safer to bring him up—like in the car. There was something about being alone with my mom in the car—the hum of the road, the feeling of being side by side but not face to face—that made hard conversations feel more possible. Less confrontational. Less fragile. So, I would test the waters. Carefully. Gently sliding in a question about him, as if I were placing something delicate on the dashboard.

I would ask, very casually, "What's his last name?"

Another time, when I was a bit older and school projects started circling around identity and heritage, I asked, "Is he Italian?"

I really, really hoped he was Italian. Italian felt romantic. Familiar. Easy to explain to classmates standing around their poster boards.

My mom smiled gently and said, "No, honey. They're Hungarian."

Hungarian.

I remember thinking, *I don't know anything about that.*

When my mom spoke about him, she was careful. Generous, even. She told me the good things first. He's very smart. He can be very charming. He's an excellent cook. There was always warmth in her voice when she said those parts.

But—there was always a *but*.

"But he is an alcoholic."

"But he's an addict."

"But he binges."

Words like "alcoholic" and "addict" floated into my childhood vocabulary long before I understood what they meant. They sounded heavy. Adult. Slightly dangerous. Like words I wasn't supposed to touch too closely. They felt ... icky. That's the only way I knew how to name it back then.

And children—especially hopeful ones—have a quiet way of editing reality to protect their hearts. So, a part of me simply hoped those things weren't really true.

When I was fourteen, my mom decided it was time. Time to reintroduce us.

I remember the nervous electricity of that first meeting—the strange familiarity of someone who I knew to be my father but emotionally was a stranger. Me, in my oversized t-shirt, still damp from an afternoon water fight in the schoolyard. Him, in his leather jacket and sunglasses, face wet from the tears that fell. I studied him carefully, the way teenagers do when they're trying to gather data quickly.

Within a fairly short time, I began to understand what my mom had been trying to prepare me for. I was only fourteen, but I had enough awareness to sense when something wasn't quite right. Nothing dramatic at first. Nothing you could easily point to and name. Just ... cracks.

I could see he was trying. I want to be very clear about that now, looking back with adult eyes. He was trying in the ways he knew how.

But there were broken promises. Lots of "We're going to do this." "We'll go here." "I'll pick you up at ..."

And then the familiar childhood scene so many children of addiction know too well: Waiting. Watching the clock. Listening for the sound of a car that doesn't come.

Sometimes there was a phone call. Sometimes an excuse. Sometimes just silence that stretched longer than it should have.

Nothing unique about our story in that way. Painfully common, actually.

Because I never lived with him, I didn't see the full extent of his struggle. And now, standing where I stand today, I can say with compassion that he probably worked very, very hard to make sure I didn't.

There were only a few moments when I saw him clearly under the influence—moments that left me flushed with embarrassment and confusion and a kind of quiet heartbreak I didn't yet have language for.

But still … I believed something very firmly back then.

My mom—in her steady, unwavering way—raised me to believe I could be anything. Do anything. That my potential was, in her words, "infinite." And I was a dreamer. Still am.

But there was one thing I was absolutely certain of as a teenager. One thing I believed with my whole chest. Whatever else my life became, I will never be *that*. I will never be an addict. I will never be an alcoholic.

Life had a way of humbling my certainties. Somewhere along the way—quietly, almost politely—my own story began to shift.

I had my first drink. And I remember it with uncomfortable clarity now, because it wasn't dark or chaotic or shame-filled the way people sometimes expect these stories to begin. It was … relief. Immediate. Warm. Exhaling-for-the-first-time relief. I remember thinking, almost with wonder, *Oh. This is what I've been missing.*

Then, I had my first drug. It felt like something inside me finally opened. Like I had suddenly found the strength to be in the world—fully, freely, without the constant second-guessing that had always lived in my chest. I could say the things I had always wanted to say. I could look people in the eye. I could feel, for the first time, genuinely connected.

For so long, I had carried this quiet loneliness I could never quite name, like I was standing just outside of life, watching it happen for everyone else. And, in that moment, it felt like I had finally stepped inside.

I didn't think of it as dangerous. I thought of it as useful. Helpful, even. Like I had finally found the thing that made being in my own skin feel … manageable.

So, of course my next thought was, *I want to feel like this as often as possible.*

Slowly, it began to weave itself into my life. At first, it felt like I was treating something. Managing something. Medicating a quiet ache I didn't yet have language for. But addiction is patient. What begins as relief eventually begins to take. And somewhere along the way—so gradually I didn't clock the exact moment—what I thought was helping an easily curable malady was quietly becoming a much bigger problem.

When I was about twenty, my father had just come out of treatment again. One of many attempts that, at the time, I didn't take very seriously. I was home from university for the weekend when my grandmother called. She said, "Your father has invited us to a meeting on Saturday night."

I remember pausing before I replied, "Oh ... okay. Sure. I'll go."

But the truth was, I didn't want to go. Not even a little bit. By then, resentment toward him had hardened in me. *What a loser*, I remember thinking. *He's ended up here. With these people.*

Still, I went.

The meeting was called Saturday Night Live—a Cocaine Anonymous meeting. I can still see it so clearly. The fluorescent lights. The folding chairs. The smell of coffee and wood.

And there he was. Standing at the door as the greeter. Little name tag on his chest. Nervous smile. Trying so hard.

Something in me recoiled.

I pulled my hat down low, hoping no one would recognize me, hoping I could somehow disappear into the back of the room. I sat there, stiff with judgement, arms folded tightly across my chest, silently separating myself from everyone I saw. *I am not like these people. I will never be like these people.*

But something unexpected happened that night. When we left, I remember feeling ... different. Not transformed. Not softened in any dramatic way. But something inside me had shifted—just slightly.

Then, life moved forward the way it does—quietly at first, and then all at once.

Six years slipped by.

I finished school. I built a life working for a big company in Toronto's financial district with glass walls and polished floors. On paper, everything looked exactly right. I was in a relationship. Living in a beautiful apartment. Traveling. Moving in circles that, from the outside, signalled success.

I remember thinking, *Okay. I've arrived.* Money. Prestige. Social calendars filled to the edges.

What I didn't understand then was that I thought I was building a big, beautiful life—something solid, something impressive, something that would finally make me ... untouchable.

*You can't hurt me. You can't hurt me,* were my quiet screams underneath it all.

So, brick by brick, I gathered the right people, the right places, the right things, stacking them carefully around me like protection.

But looking back now, I can see the truth I couldn't see then: My life wasn't getting bigger. It was getting smaller. And somewhere underneath it all, I was deeply, profoundly afraid. Afraid of the quiet. Afraid of what might surface if I ever slowed down. Afraid of the loneliness that still lived just beneath the surface of my carefully constructed life.

So, I stayed busy. I stayed moving. I stayed numb in all the ways that, for a while, still tricked people into believing I was really living.

During this time, my father was still struggling. I knew it. Even when we weren't speaking about it directly, I could feel the familiar instability around him—the starts and stops, the attempts at getting well that didn't quite hold.

Until the seizure. The one that could have been fatal if he'd been alone.

I remember the hospital visit, though parts of it now feel fogged over in a way that makes my chest tighten when I sit with it too long.

I didn't have the capacity to show up to hard things without my cocktail of courage anymore. I had started to rely so heavily on drugs and alcohol to move through life—especially anything emotionally uncomfortable—that facing something raw without that buffer felt almost impossible.

So, when I went to see him in the hospital, I went with a head full of judgement. I was also high. No, he wasn't okay. But I was. That was the story I told myself.

I remember standing there, looking at him in the hospital bed, and feeling this complicated mix of emotions I didn't yet have the maturity (even as an adult—but maybe that was just an excuse) to untangle—fear, frustration, sadness ... and if I'm being honest, superiority. Because what I couldn't see then, or maybe didn't want to see, was how my path was mirroring his.

After that health scare, something did shift for him. He became abstinent. And when I say his life began to change quickly, I mean it was noticeable. Tangible. The kind of shift you can feel even if you're still guarded.

Part of me hoped—deeply, quietly hoped—that this would be the moment our relationship finally begin to soften too. By then, it was strained in ways I couldn't yet explain. Being around him still felt ... difficult. Heavy. Unsettling. The truth was, I hadn't forgiven him—and the same illness that was taking hold of me was quietly feeding that resentment.

As he stayed sober, I spiraled. At first, it was subtle—easy to explain away, easy to minimize. But slowly, steadily, things in my life started to slip. I started losing things. Opportunities. Jobs. Momentum.

But more than that—and this is the part that still catches in my throat—I started losing people. I became the "no-show." The friend who said she'd be there ... and wasn't. The daughter who meant well but couldn't follow through. The sister they learned not to fully count on.

And the painful truth is, I knew it. I could feel the disappointment building around me, even as I kept telling myself I still had control. That I was fine. That this wasn't the same thing I had watched swallow him.

I won't go too far into the details—I've told my sobriety story many times—but eventually, everything became unmanageable.

The end didn't come all at once. It came after a seven-day binge that left my body hollowed out and my spirit threadbare. I remember drifting somewhere between sleep and consciousness, the room heavy and still. Before I even opened my eyes, I heard my sister's voice from the edge of the bed.

"My sister ... she's an addict," she spoke into the phone.

My heart dropped straight through me.

Because there it was—the truth I had spent years outrunning, finally spoken out loud. Not by me. By her.

For a moment, shame flooded in hot and fast. But right behind it came something else. Relief. Because it was true. And I was exhausted from pretending it wasn't.

I woke up in a detox centre. My sister had arranged it and brought me the night before. And somewhere deep in my body, in a place beyond the bargaining and the minimizing and the quiet little lies I'd been telling myself, I knew. This was it.

Before that, I had circled the edges of recovery. I had dipped in and out of 12-step meeting rooms. I had listened but not fully surrendered. This time was different. I was ready.

By then, I had strained so many relationships that my world had grown small and quiet. My phone wasn't exactly lighting up.

I had a small notebook with a few numbers written down. And one of them was his. For all the years of complicated history between us, I knew one thing for certain: He would pick up. And he did.

In the ways he knew how, he showed up for me. Quietly. Gently. Bringing small things like vitamins, sparkling water, little comforts he hoped might help make those early days a bit more bearable. Thoughtful things. Human things. And I was grateful. And whether either of us could fully name it yet or not, something between us was beginning to shift.

I stayed. Through detox. Then, treatment. Through the long, tender early days of learning how to be in my own skin again.

And then came ninety days. Ninety days sober.

I remember getting ready that night with a quiet kind of pride I wasn't used to feeling. Not the loud, performative kind I had chased for so many years, but something steadier. Something that came from the inside. And I knew exactly where I was going.

Saturday Night Live—the same meeting I had walked into twelve years earlier, tight and guarded, just there to support him. The memory of that first night still lived somewhere in my body. But this time, when I walked through the doors, the room didn't feel foreign. It felt warm. Familiar.

The smell hit me first—coffee and old wood and something else I can only describe as relief. The buzzing conversation. Bursts of laughter. Chairs shifting gently across the floor. This room, once filled with people I had quietly judged, had become something else entirely. It had become medicine.

And that night, I was there to pick up my ninety-day chip. This time, I knew I had earned every single one of those days.

My father came.

I remember sitting down beside him and feeling this almost surreal wave move through me. Twelve years earlier, I had walked into this very room to support him. And now he was sitting next to me, supporting me.

Life has a way of humbling you like that. Of bringing you full circle in ways you never could have planned.

And somewhere in that moment—sitting side by side in those familiar metal chairs, the room buzzing softly around us—something inside me began to soften toward him in a way it never had before. Not all at once, but enough to notice. Enough to begin.

Sobriety did something neither of us had been able to do before. It opened the door.

One afternoon, during one of our phone calls, I found myself telling him a story I had never fully admitted out loud. I don't even remember what prompted it exactly. Maybe it was the growing safety between us. Or maybe I was just finally tired of carrying it alone.

"I remember when I used to try so hard," I told him.

There was a pause on the other end of the line—the kind where you know someone is really listening.

I told him how I would go out with friends back then, back when I still believed I could manage it. Most of them could. They would go out, have a few drinks, maybe use a little, laugh, dance, and then ... go home. Go to bed. Wake up the next morning and move on with their lives as planned. I couldn't understand how they did it. Because by that point, something already had a vice grip on me. Once I started, there was no reliable off-switch. No clean stopping point. No graceful exit. It was like something in my system had already crossed a line I didn't know existed.

So, one night, I told myself, *Not tonight. Tonight is different.* I went home early. I showered. I went through the motions of taking care of myself—serums, lotions, all the small rituals that were supposed to signal a reset. I pulled on my coziest pink pyjamas. The soft ones. The safe ones. I climbed into bed, determined to stay there. I really meant it.

The moment the lights went off, my mind would not quiet. It buzzed. Restless. Loud. Unsettled in a way I couldn't soothe. I lay there trying to will myself into stillness. Trying to be normal. Trying to be someone who could just ... go to sleep.

And then—like a slingshot—I was up. Out of bed. UGG boots on. Keys in hand. Already moving toward the one place I knew the night would still be alive. The place where the people and the pace matched the momentum already building inside me.

In my pink pyjamas.

I told him how the next morning I was still at, what I would have referred to as, "the afterparty," in those fluffy pink pyjamas, shaking my head at myself. *How did this happen again? I said I wasn't going to do this. And I really meant it.*

There was a long pause on the phone after I finished. And then my father said, very quietly,

"Sweetheart ... I understand."

That was the moment. Not dramatic on the outside. No music swelling. No big declaration. But inside my body, something shifted. A weight I didn't fully know I had been carrying ... lifted. He understood. Not in theory. Not as a parent trying to comfort a daughter. He understood because that had been him, too.

In that instant, something became almost painfully clear to me: He must have tried just as hard as I had. He must have made the same promises to himself. He must have woken up in the same confusion, the same shame, the same quiet disbelief at how his own willpower kept getting outrun. And damn it, it must have absolutely crushed him to be away from me for nine years and then let me down when I was finally back in his life.

I had spent so many years believing there was this distance between us that would never close. However, in that moment, much of it did.

I didn't sit down and decide to forgive him. There was no formal process. No conscious moment of, *Okay, now I forgive you.* It was simpler than that. And deeper. Understanding walked in, and forgiveness followed quietly behind it.

Recovery—and the Twelve Steps—kept widening that opening. Not all at once. Slowly. Layer by layer. I found myself no longer carrying the same heavy resentment I once had toward him for the past. The sharp edge of it had softened into something more spacious. More honest.

That doesn't mean our relationship suddenly became easy. Life isn't that tidy. Neither is recovery. Neither are families.

My father's journey has been nothing short of miraculous in many ways. He is abstinent. He has changed. And still ... being abstinent doesn't mean we experience sobriety the same way. It doesn't mean emotional growth happens at the same pace. It doesn't mean we run off into some perfectly healed, happily-ever-after version of ourselves.

Sometimes he is still difficult to be around. Sometimes I still feel that old twist in my chest, that familiar walking-on-eggshells feeling I knew so well growing up. But here is what is different now:

The resentment no longer blocks my view.

I can see him.

I can see the effort.

I can see the limitations.

I can see the places where he is still hurting.

And—this is the part that once felt impossible—I can accept the love he is able to give me. Not the love I wished for. Not the love I once demanded. The love he actually has the capacity to offer.

That, for me, has been the greatest gift of forgiveness.

Today, I can receive the thoughtful texts. The small gestures. The moments when he shows up in the ways he knows how. I don't have to push it away. I don't have to harden myself against it.

At the same time, I have learned something equally important: Forgiveness does not mean the absence of boundaries.

I can love him and still say no.

I can accept him and still protect my peace.

I can release the past and still respond clearly to what is happening in the present.

For a long time, I believed forgiveness was supposed to be absolute—clean, total, unconditional. Like flipping a switch from hurt to healed. But that hasn't been my experience.

Forgiveness, at least for me, lives on a spectrum. There is acknowledgment. There is understanding. There is grief. There is compassion. There is acceptance—again and again and again. And sometimes, there is simply the willingness to put down what is too heavy to keep carrying.

My own addiction—the thing I once thought was the worst thing that had ever happened to me—became the doorway to understanding him. It gave me a vantage point I never could have reached through willpower or judgement alone. I know now, almost for certain, that he tried. Likely not in pink pyjamas, but he lived his own version of the same story:

That he fought.

That he likely sat in his own shame and confusion the same way I once sat in mine.

That knowing changed everything—not perfectly. Not permanently. But profoundly.

These days, when I feel the old tension rise, I return to what I know to be true: I am no longer living inside the resentment that once consumed me. I am no longer drinking or using over the pain of this relationship. I am no longer trapped in the story I once told myself about him—or about me.

I know what peace is today. And maybe that is what forgiveness has given me most of all—not a perfect relationship, not a rewritten past, not a guarantee of ease, but freedom. Enough freedom to love him as he is. Enough freedom to protect myself when I need to. Enough freedom to stop fighting ghosts that no longer need my energy.

I don't know what the future of our relationship will look like. I don't know how much either of us will continue to grow or change.

What I do know is this: I am no longer carrying what once felt unbearable. I am no longer bound to the version of this story that kept me stuck. Today, I live with more space in my heart.

And finally, I am as free as I need to be.

Tabitha Rose is the founder of Life to Paper Publishing and the Life to Paper Foundation, organizations dedicated to transforming personal stories into books that inspire healing and change. A publisher, storyteller, and community builder, she works closely with authors to bring courageous memoirs and purpose-driven nonfiction into the world. Through the Foundation, she expands that mission by bringing storytelling programs and books to hospitals, treatment centres, and communities in need—ensuring every story has the power *to write a better future*.

## FORGIVING MOM

### KIT ROBISON

I was a good kid but always a flight risk. I would leave the house unannounced and end up at a neighbour's house. Other times, I would march into the kitchen and tell Mom that I was running away to my best friend's house. I was four. As I got older, I ignored the boundaries set by my mother, like not crossing the busy four-lane street near our home. By the time I was a teenager, I was living in Tokyo; refusing to live by the rules led to epic all-day adventures, which covered the whole city—and occasionally beyond.

I was never quite like the other kids. As a toddler, when Mom put me in a Jolly Jumper—which most kids would use to self-soothe—I used so much force with my legs that it scared me. From an early age, I didn't want what other children did. Most little boys were acting out the roles they saw Dad fulfilling. Most little girls wanted to shop and care for babies. As a little boy, I wanted nothing more than to be "mother" and get a Barbie doll for Christmas. Report is, I didn't care about other kids' toys, nor did I think to show them my toys. I did, however, love to talk with adults and frequently impressed them with my thoughtful opinions. They found my ideas impressive enough to appoint me as an honourary member of the church's ministry committee. I suppose being part of church leadership was inevitable since I grew up in the church, both building and congregation, and church functions were regularly held in my home, making it a critical and constant part of my upbringing.

My mother was the ultimate teacher. When the teachers in my district went on strike, she held classes in our dining room for all the kids whose parents wanted them to attend. She made sure that I could do math out loud before entering kindergarten. She also thought that education could solve nearly any problem. My mother was "wicked smart," to quote some of my Bostonian friends. When I was a teenager, she started teaching math to those who had no facility with math at the college level. She went on to earn a master's degree in Adult Education Techniques and was teaching online by the year 2000, when online teaching was first getting started; she was designing curriculum for online teaching near the end of her life. She taught me how important education is.

My mother was not one to be crossed or ignored. However, there is only one time my mother told me that she spanked me. I had climbed out of my car seat—it was an early version that was little more than a booster seat, mostly a pad to spread the force of restraint if we were in an accident—which made staying in it dependent upon compliance. I climbed out of it and my mother, fearing for my safety, gave me a good swat across the bum. While Mom was not into corporal punishment, sometimes I might have wished she was. My mother was the queen of the lecture. She could deliver a lecture with a severity of tone and length that, in some ways, inflicted more pain than a spanking ever would have. My mother—God rest her soul—could extend a lecture to such a length that she felt would convince you to NEVER repeat the behaviour. They were so brutal that not long ago, when my father and I were talking about the severity of the lectures, he confessed that he, on some occasions, thought she had gone too far. This, however, helped to show that what she suggested was to be adopted—if only for fear of reprisal.

I was not a discipline problem and was more likely to be the teacher's pet than the class clown. I tended to get good grades, unless I got bored in class and failed to pay attention. This led to some traumatic and epic takedowns by my teachers when they assumed I knew the material. They gave me good grades despite my handing in subpar work, like the time I turned in a story despite it being illegible because my handwriting was so poor. When my mom, who was suspicious, approached the teacher about how I got an A for a story that was illegible, the teacher said that I had read it to her. Mom then, in no uncertain terms, made sure the teacher knew that I had not read the story either but had composed one out of thin air. This was an early takedown of a teacher—the first of many.

Mom had a strong sense of what was just and was willing to call it out when she felt the world had got it wrong. I had also developed a strong sense of justice, which at one point led to me suggesting to my third-grade teacher that communal punishment was unfair and, since it was obvious that I had not been a participant in the disruption, I should be exempt. This led to the traumatic experience of the class voting on whether I had to participate in the communal punishment. Their vote humiliated me, and I was punished along with the rest. It was such a bad experience that I later needed to include it in my PTSD therapy.

There were other challenges at school. I did not fit the social molds, nor did I have any implicit understanding of the social contracts. I was encouraged very much to be my own person, to dress in the colours I liked best and in any clothes I wanted. Looking back, I realize I was given free rein in the boys clothing department at the store. However, in elementary school, not fitting the mold became dangerous. Fellow students started to enforce social norms—and at times with their fists. John Brown was the chief enforcer, but he was not alone. I have distinct memories of being taunted by the other children for trying to be goofy and wearing my jacket backwards, and for loving my new dress shoes—probably Oxfords, because they had heels.

My mom and dad had my best interests at heart. Given my social and academic challenges, it was decided I should go for comprehensive testing. They thought, reasonably, that there had to be an explanation. I was diagnosed as dyslexic. My father and I have talked more recently about the assumption that smart people would figure out how to operate successfully in society. If we were going to figure it out, why saddle us with the label and challenges a deeper diagnosis would bring? So, I returned to school and was put in a special education class for socialization. This meant being pulled from class multiple times to be trained in how to fit the social mold and how to play with other kids, even those in third and fourth grade. And before you ask, yes, I went to preschool.

With no diagnosis other than dyslexia, my mother, the teacher, decided to help her child, me, learn how to fit in better. She did not want me to get beaten up and did want me to excel in life. There were lessons on how to overcome dyslexia, like reading with your finger, which I do to this day. There were attempts to provide me with normalizing hobbies, like Little League, which was an epic failure as I was more interested in the butterflies and flowers than looking skyward for the ball. Then there was the direct form of teaching about things, like forming thicker skin and not reacting to bullies. The one that hurt the most was teaching me to act and look enough like those around me so they would leave me alone. It seems reasonable enough until you consider how thoroughly I needed to subsume my identity.

Looking back, I can see that she was parenting using what, at the time, was the best knowledge about how to help a child become a well-balanced and successful person. She had read Dr. Spock, who was incredibly well regarded until his own child committed suicide. And without knowing it, my mother had figured out the positive and negative biases of applied behaviour analysis (ABA) therapy. In ABA, you reward socially positive behaviours and punish negative behaviours. Using this formula, she would help me to build what I now know was the castle to protect myself from the world, which also became my keep. She intended it for my protection and could not have seen the harm it would do.

My challenges were so great in elementary school that my parents decided to change school districts; there was no way the district we were in could provide what I needed. The house my mother loved on the street where she had built the social network that would provide friendships for the rest of her adult life was sold and we moved to a school district that would hopefully be better equipped to help me succeed. There were improvements, but the challenges continued to happen. One kid bullied me badly enough that, after a spate of physical fights, I called him on the carpet in front of the guidance counsellor. That said, what I understand forty years later is that these fights were only made worse when combined with my somewhat frequent meltdowns from being overstimulated. The child whose basic nature was to live in peace would therefore hit a fellow student with a flute case. In another incident, a young man who had started a fight was done and ready to leave when I kicked his bicycle over to finish the fight. I became a person who, at moments, appeared to be very angry at the world.

My mother—who, as I said, was not a person to be crossed, messed with, or accused of being wrong—vigorously suggested I needed to "learn to fit in enough that they will leave you alone." While she wanted to always do what was best for me, this led to a massive shift away from being my authentic self. Moving from middle school in the U.S. to high school in Japan, I perfected the persona everyone loved. I became the "preppy kid." The world reinforced the behaviours that she was encouraging, which served to reinforce the wall of the castle that I was erecting. And thus, without understanding the significance of it at the time, Pink Floyd's *The Wall* became my high school soundtrack—the album I listened to on repeat. An album that I was, in some ways, living out day to day. And so, I kept filling in the spaces in the wall, not letting anyone in to see the real me. I filled them in so well that the quirkily dressed kid from middle school became the preppy kid in high school.

While I had moments of epic meltdown and extreme violence, they started to lessen in frequency. Why they happened, I now believe, is because repression breeds deviance. Putting much of myself in the closet came at a cost. That cost at the time became drinking, smoking, and doing drugs, among other things. The other cost was the relationship with my mother that included ever greater friction, which led to fighting between us. In my head—which by this point had significant challenges from what is today known as complex post-traumatic stress disorder (CPTSD)—she was the primary cause of my problems.

Outside the house, my friends loved to party and knew I was down to do the same. My friends' parents loved me, thought I was flawless, and wondered why I would hang out with their kids, who were no doubt a bad influence on me. Inside the house, I kept my head low, tried not to say much, and tried to be at home only when necessary. I had started a spiral into an abyss. By eleventh grade, my friends would have me in suicide watch groups. In one incident, I was so out of my head that my friends called my parents to have them pick me up from a school dance. Returning home, I had a meltdown on the kitchen floor. My overwhelmed and exasperated mother, instead of getting close and trying to understand me, chose to stand, arms crossed, on the other side of the kitchen, leaving me feeling completely abandoned, while demanding I suck it up and pull myself together. Dad stood just outside the kitchen, probably sensing that anything he might try would only enflame the situation. We were the toxic combination of an overwhelmed teenager being misunderstood by an overwhelmed parent, circling an inevitable drain we didn't see.

In 1989, I started dating a person who was "not my mom," turned 18, got my ear pierced, went to rehab, got engaged, and left home, moving to the next state over and starting college. Amid this, I managed to graduate high school. For graduation, Mom asked me not to wear white socks. I, in glorious defiance, decided to wear white pants for graduation. I then asked my mother what colour socks she wanted me to wear, knowing the only answer was white. When I got my ear pierced, Mom was not pleased, mostly because I told her through her bedroom door one night after she had gone to bed. Additionally, we had previously talked about it, and she wanted to go with me because she wanted her ears to be pierced, too, but she had always been too chicken. This could have become something we did together that might have been a bonding moment.

When I got engaged, my parents thought it was an awful idea, but the comment that stuck with me most over the years was when she talked about not having previously gotten close to my girlfriend, because she was like the daughter they never had and were afraid that, like the others, she would go away.

Not long after I moved off to college, Mom and I decided to call a truce. We did not see each other often and when we did, it was often just for lunch. We did not want to spend the little precious time we had together fighting, and so we agreed not to fight when we were together. This did not resolve the tension; we simply agreed not to acknowledge it. I knew she loved me and wanted to help me, even if she had traumatized me in the process. She knew that I loved her and was a lot like her, and this antagonized her. This led to regularizing the relationship without resolving the challenges. Over the years, my mother and I continued to have a very close—some might even say fused—relationship that was never relieved of friction. I continued to move forward in life, but by this point was directing my own ship—

though still not understanding why the decisions I made never quite worked out and continuing to double down on the walls that kept traumatized-little-me safe from the world.

I worked hard at becoming the most reliable person most people knew. I became the person who always gave of myself to help others. Society rewarded me at moments when I fit into the mold and punished me when I failed to see I had violated a social contract. My mother encouraged my newfound identity as it was leading me to be a "growing and more stable" part of society. I continued to look for a way to move forward and be successful. Eventually, I found the super-conservative religious doctrines of the Non-Denominational Evangelical Pentecostal Churches. Having grown up in the church and having had the greatest social success in the church as a child, returning to the church made sense. It was also in keeping with everything my mom would do but in a "not my mom" way. The church, for its part, was happy enough to provide me with a checklist for what it meant to be a male in society.

In 1993, at the age of twenty-two, I left college, got married to my high school sweetheart, and my eldest child was born. My daughter was the fulfillment of the greatest desire of the four-year-old who only ever wanted to be "mom." As I was now fully involved in conservative church circles, I was lauded for starting my family young. I was told how to be a good father and a good husband. By 1995, I was living in the deep south and attending church every Sunday and most Wednesdays. I was meeting other people who were also part of these circles, and my second child was born. I had fully subsumed any self-understood identity to that of the dutiful father and husband. Any discomfort I had was politely ignored, and life started to look normal on the outside. I was a stable employee, loved because of my hard work and productivity. With help from my parents, my wife and I got a newer car and slowly, but steadily, experienced a level of financial success in addition to the social success I had been enjoying.

By the year 2000, when my youngest was born, the cracks were beginning to show. We had moved out of the South, and while I retained the tenants of the conservative church, we attended a more liberal Lutheran church. We were now living close to my parents, who could help with the kids at times, but who held fewer conservative views than my wife and me on parenting. I had taken a job that allowed me to become, and rewarded me for being, a workaholic. I had returned to drinking, although mostly in a controlled fashion, and I had started to use pornography in a way that was consistent with addiction. The repression—which I saw as authored by my mother—while making me socially successful, was once again breeding deviance. I was also once again beginning to hide my behaviour, as I told work I was done working and home that I was staying at work to create a pocket of time where I could breathe.

The year 2001 would be the beginning of a long journey to becoming a healthy version of myself and ultimately forgiving my mother. My wife and I knew something had to change. I was neither happy nor at peace, which led to me making the decision to go to a seminary in early 2001. Then, late in the year, I got caught using pornography at work. This was to be the first consequence of returning to addictive behaviours but also led to the first step in healing. I agreed to go to therapy, where I was asked a critical question, "Who is Kit?" I had fully subsumed my identity to the roles that I filled, and I was well loved for it. This meant that my answer was, "My wife says ... my children say ... my parents say ... and my boss says ..." but when the question was turned around to me saying who I was, I had no answer. I know now that the healthy answer comes from a self-understanding of who we are and then what we do comes out of that, but the castle walls of these roles felt like they kept me safe.

In 2003 I started eye movement desensitization and reprocessing (EMDR), a trauma therapy, to help reduce the sway that things, like getting beaten up in elementary school, had on my life. I also managed to quit smoking and got on a psych med that would help with depression and increase dopamine levels to help reduce the tendency toward addiction. As I healed some parts of myself, I experienced a lot of personal growth over a few years and had a much better understanding of how what I was doing came out of me, instead of having the things I was doing define me. Then I got ordained and returned to a rural community, slipping back into the roles that I was lauded and rewarded for fulfilling, but with a little more of myself still present. Then, in 2010, I managed to quit drinking with the help of a 12-step program and started back on the journey to healing and health.

In 2015, I had healed enough to accept those parts of myself that were like my mother, but which I hadn't liked. This was evidenced by spending most of my time that summer with someone who was a lot like my mother. I found her smart and witty and beautiful. Chi and I were both part of the same 12-step program, and so it started with conversation after meetings and over meals. It became frequent trips, just the two of us going to the art museum, the symphony, or just climbing to the top of a cathedral. The tension created by the unspoken and unacknowledged attraction between us was so strong that Olivia, a mutual friend, said out of the blue, "You should just sleep with Chi. She doesn't care that you are married." I chose not to because I was married to the person I had met and started dating in 1989. I was also the pastor of a church and needed to maintain ethical standards, but Chi still showed me the growth that had occurred.

This was also the time when I came to understand that I was transgendered, which was the next huge step on a healing journey. I had an incredible group of people around me, and I had returned to living overseas, in Ecuador, which was helping my heart to sing. I still remember this summer with great fondness. I still cherish the friendships that were made, but life was to take another left turn by forcing me to leave Ecuador.

Returning to the U.S. in 2016, I started working with a therapist who was helping me through questions about my gender. In 2017, my parents came to visit me in Miami. Mom was in remission from her Non-Hodgkin's Lymphoma and finally had the strength to travel. I tried to come out and she simply said, "Do what you want to, so long as no one else gets hurt." This phrase, I now realized, had boomeranged on me. It had become, "Do for others and always take it on the chin if it helps others, and if there is anything left, that is your portion." What it spoke to me was: the pain you experience in giving so much of yourself, in helping others and neglecting your own needs, doesn't matter. I never got to speak the words to her and Dad on that trip, that I felt the need to transition my gender. Instead, the message of "do what helps you to fit in" got retransmitted to me. Thankfully, this time I had a lot of healing under my belt and the assistance of a good therapist.

In 2018, while I was on a trip to Guyana and Suriname, I received the news that my mother had died suddenly. She was in the hospital; it was the morning after her first chemo treatment, and she and my father were talking about lunch. She had a massive heart attack and died nearly instantaneously. I understand they tried valiantly to revive her, but to no avail; she was gone in an instant. Her funeral, in keeping with someone who had been part of the church their whole life, was woven into the Sunday service on Mother's Day. I, who probably was expected to take the spot as a male matriarch of the family, abdicated the throne instead. I no longer had it in me to subsume my identity to social expectations, and nor did I want to.

Her participation in the church, even if it was a liberal church, led to my participation in church—although a much more conservative one. I now understand that all churches operate on a scale of very conservative to conservative, as is the nature of an old institution. I was always bigger than a conservative institution, and so was she. She just never felt she could leave the comfort of the institution through which she had accomplished some of her best work and from which she received the comfort of community. I have since, with some help from the institution, been able to leave it and experience the freedom of not having these externally imposed expectations.

My mother was a feminist who had suffered for being female and told what she could not do. Thus, she was proud and happy to have sons that could be taught to be fair to all and to make the world a place where she might not have been denied her deepest desires, but who had the automatic privilege not to suffer the denials she had. Thus, I was trained to use my position of power as a cisgender white male to reach back and lift others up. She was so proud of me managing to accomplish the things that she was never allowed to. I went to seminary and got ordained, which she wanted for herself. If she could not have it herself, then maybe she could work so others would in the future. She even worked on LGBTQ+ rights, because everyone should have an equal opportunity at all things.

I realize now that my mother had lived a life that served others, accepted that she could not be who she fully wanted to be; that she had parented with both love and care, but also using the best information at the time (even if it had led to trauma in me), and that she hoped the paths she led me down would keep me from being hurt or challenged in life.

Good parents want the world to be a kind and gentle place for their children, and she wanted nothing less for me. A comment from my father has confirmed she probably wouldn't have dealt well with my transitioning my gender. She was very much a "deal with the cards you are dealt" kind of person and was used to not being allowed to be the person she knew herself to be. Asking me to do the same would therefore not have seemed problematic.

What I see now that has led me since her death to forgive her is the understanding that parents want the world to be easy for their children. My path was never easy. I have received an autism diagnosis, and being on the spectrum has been compounded by the presence of attention-deficit/hyperactivity disorder (ADHD). Growing up, my mother did not know what she was working with, and the best she could do was try and help me fit in enough to not get hurt. Being transgendered but trained to fulfill the role of male in society so that I would not suffer violence was meant for good, even if it was traumatizing. There was no way for her to foresee the hurt that path would cause, and so I have chosen to forgive her, coming to believe that if she knew what I do today, things might have come together differently.

I choose to forgive her because, despite everything, I have three amazing and beautiful daughters who are making the world a better place. I also choose to forgive her because I can see how the path to becoming myself, while being challenging, has made me a strong person. It led me to live an admittedly chaotic but interesting life. I am the brilliant, quirky, weird person, working for world peace one person at a time because of the challenging journey I took, so how can I remain forever resentful of her? Today I see the ways we are similar people and hope that I live that out in a healthier way for the future of the world, with apologies to my children for the ways in which not being the person I am today, at an earlier time, harmed them.

## Epilogue

I would like to tell you that acceptance of self and forgiveness of my mother has perfectly repaired the relationship with my children. I have three adult children who, to greater and lesser extents, depending on their age, grew into adults with world views shaped by the person I was. Those relationships range from close and warm to tentative rebuilding. Any of these might well not exist at all if I had not done the work to get to where I am. The rebuilding is complicated by the combination of me being an addict in recovery and them now caring for the spouse I eventually divorced.

Some of the damage done was a loss of confidence in me as an honest broker. As an active addict, I was not an honest person, and this confidence can only be rebuilt by being an honest person over the course of time. However, forgiveness of my mother has been key to allowing me to accept my part in their trauma and world view. I am now working to rebuild from a place of honesty. I am proud to say that they are all working to heal their trauma—personal and generational. I would like to believe that I have been an example of the same for them and that, with time, I might have a warm relationship with each of them.

Kit is a queer, neurodiverse, third-culture, nomadic, transgender woman, who lives in a van and travels the world, working for world peace, one person at a time. Many know her as Pink Pastor, a teacher and spiritual guide.

# AS WE FORGIVE THOSE WHO TRESPASS AGAINST US

SUSAN RAPHAEL

For the one still holding the pain, we whisper the words so easily, don't we?

"As we forgive those who trespass against us."

I, for one, used to say them in church as a little girl. Looking back, I wonder if I ever understood what those words meant. As an adult, I remain curious about these words, often said by rote, without conviction. Do we actually believe we can forgive those who do us wrong? Maybe in the sanctity of a church, but not in the real world. I prefer to live my life informed by spiritual principles rather than the tenets of organized religion. Yet, when I sat at my desk to write this story, those indelible words came to me, once again.

But what happens when those words get stuck in your throat? When you want to forgive—you really do—but the wound is still raw? When the trespass didn't feel like a small thing, but a deep violation of trust, of safety, of love?

This story is for those who are still in pain. The ones who haven't found the forgiveness they need. The ones who want peace but don't know how to get there. The ones who feel ashamed for not being further along. I want to share with you that you are not failing—*You are grieving.*

Forgiveness isn't the finish line, I am learning. It's not proof of my strength or of my faith. It's not a single decision you make and then move on.

It's a path—sometimes slow, sometimes hidden—that winds through grief, anger, disbelief, betrayal, and exhaustion. And some days, that path feels entirely blocked.

I have sat across from many people in pain. Parents whose children won't speak to them, or worse, their child has died. Survivors of betrayal. People harmed by those they were told to trust. And I've heard this one truth echo again and again: "I want to forgive, but I can't."

To them, I say, "Then don't forgive, not yet." Not because forgiveness doesn't matter, but because your pain matters, too. You don't need to bypass any of your feelings for some "greater good." You don't need to pretend you're ready. Forgiveness that is forced becomes another kind of betrayal—this time against yourself.

The line from the prayer reads, "as we forgive," not "as we perform forgiveness." It suggests a process, not a product; a way of being in the world, not a rule to obey under pressure.

Forgiveness, when it comes, rarely looks the way we expect. I have forgiven people while asleep and dreaming. And I've awoken with a sense of peace.

It doesn't mean the pain disappears. It doesn't mean trust is restored. Sometimes, it doesn't even mean reconciliation. What it does mean—what it can mean—is that we stop allowing what someone else did shape who we are. It means we are no longer tethered to the trespass. It means we are making room in our hearts for something other than the wound.

Forgiveness envelops us, not because we're strong enough, but because something soft and sacred finds us when we finally stop gripping the pain so tightly. And when it comes, we don't feel victorious—we feel relieved. We feel human again.

If you're not there yet, you are not lost. You are just on the way. And the way takes time.

So, for today, don't force forgiveness. Hold yourself with gentleness. Tell the truth about your pain, and trust that healing can happen even in the waiting.

## The Weight of Unforgiven Grief

> In the process of forgiveness, it is not always the person we forgive who benefits. Sometimes, it's us who are saved from carrying the burden of anger and bitterness.
>
> SUSAN RAPHAEL

> Life becomes easier when you learn to accept an apology you never got.
>
> ROBERT BRAULT

Forgiveness. The word seems so simple, yet for many of us, it's anything but. It's a journey, one that takes time, effort, and, most importantly, emotional vulnerability. When I first embarked on the path of recovery from alcohol addiction, I had no idea what was waiting for me. I thought the work was about abstaining from substances. But as I soon discovered, it was about so much more than just that.

For the first time in my life, I would experience emotions in a way I never had before—raw, unmedicated, and unfiltered. Let me tell you, it was both a beautiful and terrifying experience. For so long, I had used substances to numb myself, to avoid the sharp sting of my true feelings. But when those substances were removed from my life, I was left with nothing but myself and the tidal wave of emotions I had spent years suppressing.

And then came William.

My first romantic relationship in recovery was unlike anything I had ever experienced. It was new. It was exciting. But it was also overwhelming in ways I wasn't prepared for. I had never felt feelings so intensely, so purely, without the veil of numbing substances. I was learning to navigate emotions like love, fear, vulnerability, and even heartbreak—all for the first time.

I had never known what it felt like to be truly present with my own emotions. I had spent years avoiding them through drugs and alcohol, always running from myself. But in recovery, I was forced to face the truth of who I was without the crutch of substances. And that truth was both beautiful and painful.

When William entered my life, it felt like a breath of fresh air. His energy, his presence, his laughter—everything about him was captivating. We shared a connection that felt special, one that we both believed was destined to last. For the first time, I felt things I had never experienced. And we shared recovery. He made me feel alive, and there was chemistry. But alongside the highs of this connection, there were also the lows—the doubts, the fears, and the uncertainty that came with trying to navigate a relationship while navigating my own recovery. One of my mentors reminded me that chemistry can blow things up!

In those early days, I didn't know what was happening inside of me. I felt this rush of emotions—joy, excitement, vulnerability—and I couldn't make sense of them all. But as I got deeper into the relationship, I began to realize that these feelings were also terrifying. The rawness of my emotions was almost too much to handle. I had never known love without some form of escape. I had never known what it was like to truly feel without trying to run away from it.

And then, of course, came the reality of dating someone else in recovery.

William had just come back into recovery from a relapse when we met. He got sober very young and had been sober for several years when he relapsed. Although I was told time and time again by mentors and fellow members of the recovery community that dating someone when I was in early recovery wasn't advisable, I ignored the warnings. I waited until I had almost one year of recovery, after all. And I told myself that William wasn't really in early recovery. He had done this before; he had been sober for years. I rationalized everything. After all, we had such a strong connection. And didn't I deserve to feel loved? Didn't I deserve this happiness?

But what I didn't understand at the time was that recovery isn't linear. It's not a straight path that you walk and then, suddenly, you're healed. It's messy. It's full of setbacks and relapses, and that's something I was about to learn the hard way.

William and I quickly fell into a pattern of highs and lows. When things were good, they were great. We would laugh together, cook meals, and go out on spontaneous adventures. But when things were bad, they were devastating. William's recovery was fragile, and when the pattern of relapse set in, it felt like the ground beneath me was pulled away.

I had never known what it felt like to deal with someone else's addiction without being actively addicted myself. I had spent years in my active addiction, lost in the chaos, and I hadn't been equipped with the tools to handle someone else's struggles. In my early recovery, I was still learning how to stay sober, how to deal with the deep emotions I was feeling. How could I help him if I couldn't even fully help myself?

But there was something in me that refused to let go. Something that made me think I could fix him, that if I loved him enough, if I was patient enough, everything would be okay. But what I failed to realize was that I couldn't heal him. I couldn't fix his addiction. And in trying to do so, I was only distracting myself from my own healing.

The emotional turmoil took its toll. I felt like I was constantly on a rollercoaster. I would spend days worrying about where he was, if he was using again, why he lied, what his next move would be. And each time he disappeared, I was left in a pit of fear and confusion. It was like I couldn't breathe, couldn't think straight. I was addicted to the chaos of it all, even as I was building a sober life for myself.

The hardest part was the emotional pain I felt every time he would pull away. I felt so helpless. I had never faced heartbreak while sober before. In the past, I had always turned to substances to numb the pain, to avoid feeling it. But this time, I couldn't escape it. I had to sit with the discomfort, the fear, and the uncertainty. And it hurt. I desperately wanted to kill the pain. Yet, I did not pick up a drink. I stayed sober and endured the pain.

And while I struggled to make sense of my emotions, I also found myself questioning who I was in this relationship. Was I being too lenient? Was I enabling his behaviour? Or was I simply loving someone who was hurting, someone who needed support? I had no clear answers. All I knew was that I was desperately caught up in something with him, even as I could see the cracks in our relationship forming.

It wasn't until I sought help from Al-Anon and codependency programs that I began to see things more clearly. I had always focused on my own struggles in recovery, but this was the first time I was able to truly look at how addiction had affected those around me—how my behaviours while in addiction had hurt the people I loved. I realized that I wasn't just dealing with William's addiction; I was also grappling with my own codependence and my need to fix things that were beyond my control.

This was the turning point. This was when I started to learn about true forgiveness—not as something I was doing for William, but as something I had to do for myself. I had to let go of the idea that I could control his recovery. I had to forgive him for things he hadn't even apologized for. And I had to forgive myself for holding on to something that wasn't serving either of us.

The truth was, I couldn't continue to hold on to resentment and bitterness. The only one I was hurting was myself. Holding onto my pain was like drinking poison and hoping it would hurt him. I had to let it go—if not for him, then for me.

One day, something shifted. I was waiting outside a recovery meeting when I heard that William had relapsed again. But this time, something changed in me. I felt an overwhelming sense of forgiveness. I realized that my anger—my resentment—had been misplaced. I had been so focused on my own hurt that I had lost sight of the fact that William was struggling with a life-threatening disease. We had the same disease, and yet he was in it, and I had, but for the grace of God, grasped onto a life preserver, one day at a time.

This realization was like a weight lifted off my shoulders. For the first time, I felt free. Free from resentment, free from pain. I didn't have to carry it anymore. Forgiveness washed over me like a wave, and I knew, deep down, that I had finally let go.

The funny thing about forgiveness is that it's not something we control. It's not something we can force. It envelops us when we are ready to accept it. It is a gift that we give to ourselves, not to the other person.

I didn't realize how heavy the burden of resentment was until it was gone. It's like carrying weight on your shoulders for so long that you forget what it feels like to stand tall without it. But once the weight is lifted, you stand up straighter, breathe easier, and see the world differently.

Some months after I ended things with William, I ran into a childhood friend I hadn't seen in years. She asked if I was dating anyone and then suggested I meet someone special she knew; she thought we might hit it off. Despite feeling a little hesitant, I took a chance and met her friend some weeks later for a blind date.

This special someone eventually became my husband. I had no idea at the time that letting go of William and forgiving him for what he couldn't be was the first step toward finding someone who could show up for me in ways I had always dreamed of.

One winter day, during the COVID-19 pandemic, twenty-some odd years after last seeing William, I had a strange encounter that forced me to reckon with everything once again. I was driving through the city, running a few errands on a cold afternoon. I was frustrated because I had to return something to a post office several blocks from my house. It was one of those small, ordinary tasks that felt unnecessarily irritating. As I sat at a stoplight, my mind was lost in the mundane details of the day; then, I saw him.

William—I noticed him right away. He was standing on a street corner. His face was unshaven, his clothes worn and disheveled, and his eyes—those eyes I once adored—had a distant, hollow look. He was panhandling.

The image hit me like a punch to the gut. I felt my heart tighten as a wave of emotion washed over me. There he was—the man I had loved—standing in the same city I lived in, reduced to asking for spare change. It was as though the pain I had carried came crashing back, but with an added intensity. Seeing him like this, in such a state of despair, was far harder than I had imagined. It felt so real, so raw, in a way that I had not expected.

Tears welled up in my eyes, but I couldn't explain why. It was not just sorrow for him, but also for the unspoken grief I had carried for so long. I thought about his potential, the man he could have been, the man I once believed he was. I thought about my struggles and how far I had come. I was filled with gratitude for my recovery, for the life I had built; yet, seeing him like that brought so much sadness to the surface.

As I sat there at the red light, something unexpected happened. I felt a deep sense of compassion wash over me—compassion for him, yes, but also for myself. The anger, the resentment, the bitterness that I had held on to for so long all began to melt away in that moment. In that brief encounter, I realized that forgiveness was not just something I had to offer William; it was something I had to give to myself. Seeing him on that street corner made it clear to me that holding on to anger and resentment was only holding me back. My self-righteousness, my pride in thinking I had been wronged, was a weight I had been carrying for too long.

I drove away that day feeling something I hadn't expected: a profound sense of release. It was like the weight I had been dragging around was suddenly gone, leaving me lighter—freer. It was a form of forgiveness, not for him, but for me. It was the moment I truly understood that forgiveness isn't just about making peace with others. It's about freeing yourself from the shackles of anger and disappointment.

Forgiveness is not for the other person; it is for you. It is for your own healing. And in the end, that is the most powerful gift you can give yourself.

Years later, I learned that William had passed away from a drug overdose. He was only fifty-five. He had lived a life full of promise, but also one filled with demons. I felt a pang of sadness, but it wasn't sadness for the relationship we never had. It was for the pain he had carried, the loss he had faced, and the hope he never fully realized. And I felt a deep sense of gratitude for the recovery path I embark on one day at a time.

Forgiveness is not about excusing someone's actions. It is not about making them right. It is about finding peace within yourself. It is about freeing yourself from the chains of resentment, anger, and bitterness. And in doing so, it is about finding your own liberation.

*Two things can be true at the same time: I can love from a distance, and I can forgive.*

## Author's Note

As I continue to walk the path of recovery, I share my story in hopes that it might help others. If you are struggling, know that forgiveness is a journey, not a destination. It's one step at a time.

I am a clinician, author, and speaker specializing in teenage addiction, mental health, and family healing. The title of my book is *What's Wrong with My Teen? Finding Answers to Teenage Addiction and Family Crisis.* It is a step-by-step guide for parents navigating crisis and recovery, offering clinical insight alongside lived experience from my life and work.

Susan Raphael is a certified addiction and mental health clinician, a referral clinician with the NBA's Clinicians' Network, and author of *What's Wrong with My Teen?* Drawing on lived experience, she supports families with compassion, clarity, and real-world recovery guidance.

# TODAY, I CHOOSE

MAYA NOOR

## Childhood

I am sitting in our shared bedroom with my two older sisters, playing with our dolls. The door is closed; it is quiet and pleasant. I am smiling and happy. I love playing with my sisters. They don't always let me play with them, so this is a meaningful moment for me. I love playing with my doll. I love brushing her golden hair and pretending that she has the best life ever. A life full of happiness and joy.

Suddenly, the door bursts open; the handle smashes into the wall. My mother storms in, her face flushed red, her eyes wide and wild. I don't know what is going on, but I recognize that look. It meant the peaceful, happy moment is coming to an end. The red face and wild eyes mean I have to brace myself, for the monster is out and something bad is about to happen.

Is she coming for me this time? Or my sisters? What I did know is that I had to prepare myself for a potential attack. I hear words coming out of the monster's mouth, but my mind is too busy preparing my body to fend off the attack to comprehend what the monster was saying. My body stiffens. My breathing gets heavier and heavier the closer she comes. I start to shrink into a protective ball. The words continue to fly out of her mouth. My mind braces for impact.

She turns to one of the beds, where a school textbook is lying. She grabs the textbook and strikes me across the face with all her might. As she lifts her arm to strike again, I quickly raise mine to protect my face. This time her blow lands on my arm. Then another on my back. Then to the top of my head. Then my arm, shoulder, and back. I shrink further into a ball to protect myself. Then I hear a hit, but don't feel it. I peek through my arms and see that the monster has moved to my sister, hitting her hard. I continue to brace myself in case she comes back for another round. She then moves to my second sister. I remain where I am, alert. She stops the hitting, but more incomprehensible words are coming out of her mouth. She throws the textbook back on the bed and stomps out of the room, leaving the door wide open behind her.

There is a long moment of silence as I sit on the floor, welcoming the wave of silence after the storm. The silence goes on long enough for me to know the raging episode is over and my sisters and me are safe—for now. My body begins to slowly soften. My muscles begin to relax. My senses start to function normally again. I feel dampness on my cheeks, telling me that I had been crying. I didn't feel them in the heat of the moment. My sisters and I look at each other in silence. No words are exchanged. We telepathically acknowledge the episode is over and we are safe. Words aren't helpful during these moments. Silence is what we have always needed to restore our senses. We play with our dolls again, but it isn't the same. It is us pretending that what just happened didn't happen. Pretending that our life is normal. Pretending that we didn't experience the monster's wrath. We've been through this so many times and we know that it is better to pretend that it didn't happen than try to comprehend what just happened and why.

## Teenagerhood

I wonder if he likes me back. I think we have a connection; I know that he likes talking to me too. But why does he like talking to me? I love sharing things with him. When something funny happens in class, he's the first person I look at to see his reaction, and I usually catch him looking at me first. He's my best friend, but I think I love him, too. Does he love me? I don't know. I don't think so. I mean, why would he? I'm so ugly; Mom says it all the time. I'm sure he thinks so too. But ugly people can also be loved. I saw a woman once who wasn't conventionally beautiful—her teeth stuck out; she couldn't even close her mouth fully. And yet, she was pregnant, married, loved. So maybe, just maybe, someone ugly like me could be loved too, right? I mean, ugly people deserve to be loved too ... right?

## Adulthood

Me: "I don't like the way I am. I don't like that I struggle to speak in front of large groups of people without feeling terrified. It's not just being nervous on stage, I literally felt terrified—like I am being attacked. I am unable to remember anything I had prepared. My mind goes completely blank, and I find myself just reading the bullet points on the slide. I had prepared and practiced so much, and it was all for nothing. I don't understand why this happens to me. I hate it. I hate that I'm like that. Why can't I be normal? Why can't I present normally like everyone else? What's wrong with me?"

Therapist: "How do you feel when you're standing on stage?"

Me: "I feel numb and frozen. My body freezes, like I have no control over it. I unconsciously fold my arms in front of me; I don't know why. I feel that my mind is too busy trying to protect me, but why? There's no danger. It's just a presentation in front of some people I already know."

Therapist: "What goes on in your mind when you're up there?"

Me: "My mind goes somewhere else, like a different place from where I am. It's like it has its own escape hatch. I'm trying to remember my lines, but my mind is focused on the lights and the people, like it's scanning the room waiting for something bad to happen. And I can't control it. It's like it takes over me and I can't get it to focus on my speech. And I end up reading off the screen because my mind is refusing to think. Is this normal? Because it doesn't sound normal to me."

Therapist: "How does your body feel in that moment?"

Me: "It feels like it's in a danger zone. My body freezes and I can't get it to relax. My body does things on its own, like right when I want to open my mouth to start speaking, my arms suddenly fold of their own volition. That's not how I want to present, but my arms become so locked up that I can't get them to unlock. It actually feels safer, to be honest, with arms folded. But it doesn't look good to the audience. It's not good posture. It doesn't send the right message; it doesn't say that I'm confident in what I'm saying. Can people tell that I am nervous? That I am unable to deliver what I have prepared. It's only when I leave the stage and I'm away from the spotlight that I start feeling my body relax. When I'm back in my seat in the audience, I start feeling my breath returning to normal. I don't even realize I am breathing heavily while presenting. Why can't I relax?"

Therapist: "I want you to close your eyes and see yourself on that stage—see yourself standing there about to speak. Let yourself feel everything that you feel when you're on the stage. Let me know when you're there."

Me: "I'm there."

Therapist: "Now, go back in time to when you were a child and felt these feelings. Let me know when you're there."

Me: "I'm there."

Therapist: "Where are you and what is happening?"

I realized with a surge of anger, that my present struggles are rooted in my past. The lack of confidence, the feeling of not being good enough, the need to hide to feel safe, the lack of self-love—all trace back to my parents. They raised me to be a weak, helpless child with no self-esteem.

For so much of my lifetime feeling depressed, hopeless, unloved, unworthy. Never hating myself but hating my personality. My weakness. Feeling like a victim trapped in a dark cage, unable to see a way out. But now ... now I am angry.

I am angry with whom they have made me. I am angry they caused me to become a person I do not like. I am angry they made me doubt myself. I am angry they broke me into pieces. I am angry they are the worst parents. I am angry at what I could've become if they were not who they are.

Anger feels good. Anger gives me strength. Anger makes me feel again. Anger gives me courage. Anger makes me a person who can stand up for herself. I am no longer afraid of speaking up. I am no longer afraid of saying no. I am no longer afraid of calling them out. I am no longer allowing them to treat me the way they've been treating me. I am no longer the old me.

## Reaction

"You've changed."

"Of course, I've changed. I've grown and I'm no longer tolerating disrespect."

"You weren't like this. You used to be a better listener. Now I can't say something to you without the conversation turning into an argument."

"I wasn't a good listener. I was keeping quiet to avoid causing problems. I will no longer silence myself. If I have something to say, I'm going to say it."

"I don't know how to deal with your new personality."

"You'll learn to."

"You were easy to talk to and now I have to think twice before opening my mouth around you; even Mom was saying the same thing the other day. Everyone is wondering what happened to you. What changed? It's like you just woke up one day with this new personality; I don't get it."

"I've been treated like a doormat ever since I was born, and I'm no longer playing that role. If you want to speak to me, you speak to me with respect or don't speak to me at all."

## Resistance

"You need to forgive your parents. They did the best they can."

My body flushes with heat. My breathing grows heavier. My throat tightens. Anger rises in my chest. *I will not let myself cry,* I think, as I urge myself not to cry.

My heart aches with pain. When will anyone think of me? When will they see me? When will they hear me? When will they see that I'm the one who's hurting—that I'm the one who is suffering? Why do I have to be the one to forgive? And forgive what? The torture? The belittling? The humiliation? The discouragement? The lack of love?

They don't deserve my forgiveness, and I deserve to be angry and resentful. For everything they did to me. For everything I went through. For deceiving me into thinking that it was normal and that they are great parents. For guilt-tripping me. For manipulating me into submission and loyalty.

The one thing—everything I ever wanted from my parents—was love. I wanted to feel loved. I wanted to feel supported. I wanted to feel worthy. I wanted to feel like I matter. I wanted to feel safe. I wanted to feel protected. I wanted to feel that I was part of a unit, one full of love, peace, and harmony. All I ever wanted was to live a happy, healthy, peaceful, joyful life. Why couldn't they give that to me? Why couldn't they be who I needed them to be?

## Turning Point

> Me: *Why did this happen to me? If I really chose this life, why did I choose this? Why did I choose to be born into an abusive family?*
>
> God: *You came into this world for the experience. You went through an experience that had its challenges, where you were able to learn how to navigate and overcome it, then share the learnings and personal experience with others.*
>
> Me: *Why did I choose this horrible experience? I feel so tired and exhausted. It's too much. I don't know if I can continue with this.*
>
> God: *You have the strength to live through anything. You have the strength to endure, you have the ability to find*

*courage, to be put in a situation where all the odds are against you and still find the power within you to stand up tall for what is right. You came here to showcase the ability one has to connect with the power within to change their life for the better. To go from living in darkness to living in light. You are here to live through the process of being born into a dysfunctional environment, living through chaos, freeing yourself from the invisible handcuffs, and regaining your power to live the life you were meant to live. You are here to showcase how one can find peace and harmony in the midst of chaos.*

Me: *Why were my parents abusive? Why were they not able to be loving, gentle parents who provide a healthy, supportive environment for their children to thrive in this world? Did they not want to, or did they not know how?*

God: *Every person comes into this world to serve a purpose. A person's purpose and mission are not shared with anyone else; it is only for the individual to know. What your parents' mission and purpose on this planet are is for them to know and work on. Your purpose is to focus on your own mission. Sometimes, people take on missions and struggle to achieve their goal. And that's okay. The world is a place for growth and development—to learn and re-learn. We cannot blame others for struggling with their own mission. You also don't know what their mission is. For all you know, they may have served their mission well. Your mission is to show people how to get from darkness to light. To be able to do that, you needed to go through that experience yourself, to then be able to talk about it with firsthand knowledge. You have all the qualities and skills needed to do that. You had faith you would be able to take this task on, and you have done so successfully. It is now time for you to share your expe-*

*rience—to show others how they can do it, too. It is time to remind people that they have everything they need within them to overcome any challenge and achieve any goal.*

Me: *So, my parents chose to be abusive parents?*

God: *Your parents grew up in darkness, just like you did. They wanted to find the light, and sometimes they did, and sometimes they struggled to stay connected. The pressure around them contributed to their continued illusion of disconnection from Source. At times, humans are too influenced by society and certain programming to be able to let go of the illusion. We understand that this is not an easy task, and we understand that every person will take their experience to the extent they can; you all contribute to this world in your own ways. You came into this world with an understanding of where your parents were on their journey and chose to show them how to go from darkness to light—something that they have, consciously or subconsciously, strived to do. We cannot blame others for not achieving what we were able to achieve. For all you know, they may have achieved what they needed to achieve in this lifetime.*

Me: *Wouldn't my life have been much more pleasant if I had healthy, loving parents? Wouldn't I have had a happier and more productive life? Wouldn't I have been able to achieve much more? Imagine if I had the sense of safety and confidence to do all the things I want to do. Wouldn't I have been a better contributor to this world?*

God: *Words do not teach; life experience does. To be a courageous person, you go through an experience that causes you to stand up and be courageous. To be a kind person, you go through an experience where you're able to choose cruelty, but instead you show kindness. To be strong, you go through challenges that will help you build your strength. To be loving, you go through the experience of lacking love to then be able to sense what love is. To appreciate abundance, you need to experience scarcity. To be the person you are today, you needed to go through experiences that built the skills and qualities you have today. Despite the lack of love, you chose to be loving. Despite the control, you chose to be free. Despite the darkness that surrounded you, you chose to find the light within you. Life is a game of challenges, and you have everything you need within you to overcome every single challenge that comes your way. All you need to do is tap into the resources within you.*

Me: *So, where do I go from here?*

God: *Take the lessons, learn from them, apply them, and share your experiences with those who could benefit from them. You are here to be an example of what can be achieved. Find your strength, and those around you will find theirs. Be a beacon of light; shine your light onto darkness, and the darkness will fade away. You are not here to blame, you are here to showcase what is possible.*

Me: *Thank you, God, for all your support. I now understand what I need to do.*

God: *You are welcome.*

## Forgiveness Prayer

*I forgive myself for being too hard on myself.*
*I forgive myself for not standing up for myself.*
*I forgive myself for the times when I gave up.*
*I forgive myself for the times I put myself last.*

*I forgive myself for blaming others.*
*I forgive myself for forgetting who I am.*
*I forgive myself for times when I felt disconnected.*
*I forgive myself for thinking I was weak.*

*I forgive myself for not taking accountability.*
*I forgive myself for the times when I didn't listen to my intuition.*
*I forgive myself for the times I didn't feel strong.*
*I forgive myself for the times when I felt off-track.*

*I forgive my parents for not being who I wanted them to be.*
*I forgive my parents for not knowing more than they knew.*
*I forgive my parents for not healing from their own trauma.*
*I forgive my parents for blaming me.*

*I forgive my parents for times when they thought they did their best.*
*I forgive my parents for not listening to me.*
*I forgive my parents for not letting me speak.*
*I forgive my parents for thinking they were better.*

*I forgive my parents for hiding behind their masks.*

*I forgive my parents for not having emotional control.*
*I forgive my parents for not having the education I had.*
*I forgive my parents for the moments they seemed disconnected from Source.*

## Closure

Dear Mom,

I am writing this letter to let you know that I am releasing all the pain, the hurt, the neglect, and the longing for love I carried for so many years.

From the time I was very young, I longed for your love and acceptance. You were my mother, and all I wanted was to be seen—to feel that I mattered, to know that I was cherished. Every gift, every kind word, every attempt I made was my way of reaching for you, hoping you would reach back.

For a long time, I felt angry that this never happened in the way I needed. Angry that you could not be the mother I longed for. Angry that you could not love me in the way I dreamed of being loved. That anger lived inside me for years.

But now, I am ready to let that anger go. I see now that you were also carrying wounds. Wounds from your own childhood and adulthood that shaped how you acted in this world. Like a puppy with a thorn in its paw, you were in pain, and that pain often spilled into those around you. I understand now that your words and actions were less about me and more about the pain you didn't know how to heal.

I see that you did not have the tools, knowledge, or support to process your emotions in healthier ways. When you called me ugly, it was because you were self-loathing. When you called me a whore, it was because you were feeling guilty for your infidelities. When you told me that no one will ever love me, it was because you felt unlovable. I understand that you were doing what you could to survive in the life that you had created. It wasn't personal, even though it felt so deeply personal at the time.

I also see now that my journey had a larger purpose. Through experiencing darkness, I learned to find my own light. Through knowing the ache of unmet love, I learned to treasure the love I now receive. Through struggle, I found strength and faith. What once felt like punishment has become my greatest teacher.

I no longer see myself as a victim. I know that God gave me the strength to walk through this, not only to heal myself but to help others who may be walking their own path through pain. In that way, you, too, have been part of my purpose.

So, today, I choose to let go of blame, resentment, and sorrow. I choose instead to open my heart to compassion, forgiveness, and gratitude for the lessons I have gained. I forgive you, and I forgive myself for carrying this burden for so long.

Thank you for showing me darkness, so that I could truly appreciate the light. Thank you for showing me the absence of love, so I could embrace unconditional love when it came. Thank you for helping me, in your own way, become strong, determined, kind, and loving.

I love you, I forgive you, and I set you free.

Love,

Maya

Maya Noor is an advocate dedicated to raising awareness about narcissistic parenting and its long-term impact on adult children. Drawing from her own lived experience of being raised by a narcissistic parent, she brings both personal insight and a compassionate voice to the conversation on healing and growth.

# COMING HOME TO MYSELF

MEG NOCERO

---

> It's no use going back to yesterday, because I was a different person then.
>
> Lewis Carroll, *Alice in Wonderland*

---

## I. Sitting Here: The Beginning of Self-Forgiveness

This line has stayed with me, echoing in the quiet corners of my heart. It reminds me that I am not who I once was. The mistakes, missteps, and moments I wish I could erase were made by a version of me that no longer exists. That is the paradox.

I'm learning that forgiveness means different things to different people. But at its core, it is an intentional act—a conscious choice to release resentment and anger—not because the pain didn't happen but because we deserve peace more than punishment. There comes a moment in every healing journey when we must face not what others have done to us, but what we have done to ourselves.

The sharp words we whisper in the mirror. The dreams we dismiss before giving them a chance. The moments we abandon ourselves in the name of perfection, productivity, or people-pleasing.

Self-forgiveness is not a luxury—it is a necessity. Without it, we carry a weight we were never meant to bear. We become our own captors, punishing ourselves for being human.

Sitting here writing this ... this is how I fully and intentionally continue my journey of self-forgiveness. Not with fanfare. Not with a neat conclusion or a polished insight. But with a trembling hand, a whole heart, and the courage to face the question:

*Am I forgiving myself for what I've done—for what I've failed to do—or for believing what others unknowingly passed down?*

The truth is: for all of it, or maybe none. Because self-forgiveness isn't always logical. It's emotional. It's spiritual. It lives between regret and grace, between holding on and letting go. Today—right now, as I type these words—I choose to lay the first brick of this path. Not tomorrow. Not next week when I "feel better." Now.

In the stillness of this reckoning, I engage a sacred practice—a gentle balm passed down through generations of wisdom-keepers from the islands of Hawaii: *Hoʻoponopono.*

Pronounced ho-oh-pono-pono, this ancient Hawaiian method of reconciliation and forgiveness translates simply to "correction." At its heart, it's a process of restoring harmony—between people, within families, and, most powerfully, within ourselves. Traditionally practiced by Indigenous Hawaiian healers, Hoʻoponopono was often a communal act—an extended family sitting together to air grievances, take responsibility, and return to love. But in our modern lives, it offers something equally profound: a personal path to inner peace.

. . .

The practice is centered around four simple phrases. Four keys that can unlock even the most tightly wound guilt and shame:*

*I'm sorry. Please forgive me. Thank you. I love you.*

Each phrase can become a prayer, a melody repeated like waves over a shore, softening the jagged edges of self-judgement. Working on self-forgiveness lessens that past trauma's grip on your life. It reclaims your power and, perhaps most radically, it allows you to evolve; it allows for acceptance and love.

This feels like a key affirmation that has me reframing the past so a new journey can begin, not with forgetting, but with remembering—through the lens of compassion. This is the moment I begin to come home to myself, address my pain, and release its hold on my life. This is where a new story, couched in *freedom from* transforms to *freedom to begin*.

## II. The Wound Beneath the Smile: Childhood Narratives that Shaped Me

I was a girl who felt deeply. A girl who was told, in subtle and not-so-subtle ways, that her sensitivity was a flaw. That she was too much. That her emotions were too loud. That her brightness—her presence—was not welcome. And eventually, I started to believe it.

I don't remember exactly when the shift happened, but I remember the feeling—the shrinking, the carefulness. The way I began to tiptoe through the world, anticipating rejection before it even came. I became a master of preemptive disappointment, convincing myself not to try, not to ask, not to hope—because I didn't want to get hurt. I was bullied. Made fun of. Dismissed. Not always violently, but consistently.

---

* "Embrace Ho'oponopono: The Key to Achieving a Life of Zero Limits," Insight Aisle. https://insightaisle.com/embrace-hooponopono-the-key-to-achieving-a-life-of-zero-limits/

Death by a thousand paper cuts.

The belief—that quiet, corrosive belief—that something was wrong with me. That I was fundamentally flawed and not worthy of love became the narrative that played like a loop in my mind. I didn't know how to stop it. I didn't realize it was a lie; so, I internalized it as truth. And that truth became a self-fulfilling prophecy during those years of early development.

I entered rooms already apologizing for my presence. I dimmed my light before anyone asked me to. I chose people who confirmed my unworthiness. I created circumstances where my fear of rejection was realized, just so I could say, "See? I knew it."

The punishment I thought I deserved—emotional exile and loneliness—I administered it myself. Because I thought that was what love required:

*Shrink to be accepted. Silence to be safe. Sacrifice your voice to belong. And oh, how I longed to belong.*

I remember a lot of sadness. Not that I allowed the world to know. I became skilled at hiding it—behind a smile that said "I'm fine" when I wasn't. But underneath that smile lived a wounded little girl.

As a kid, my life often felt out of control. And when the world feels unsafe, we find ways—any ways—to cope. Mine started early.

In second grade, I got braces. My teeth were crooked, and so were the comments from my peers. The teasing was relentless, and I couldn't escape it—not at school, not in my own head. I learned to numb myself with food. It became a comfort. It became protection. It became my first addiction. Even now, I still carry those triggers—the haunting echoes of shame I thought I had outgrown. They're embedded in my psyche, wired into my nervous system. When life feels overwhelming, I still sometimes hear the old voice:

*Fix yourself. Control something. Be better or disappear.*

I never had a positive body image. Not really.

My parents were loving in many ways, but also intensely self-critical. They inherited their own shame and passed it down in subtle ways—offhand remarks, diet talk, comments about weight that seemed harmless but weren't. Eventually, I turned from food to control.

I starved myself for days. I even flirted with bulimia. Then, I created an order through exercise.

Working out became my sanctuary, my structure. I used it to regulate my emotions, my weight, my self-worth. When I exercised, I felt powerful; when I didn't, I felt like I was failing. It gave me a sense of mastery over chaos. And in many ways, it helped me build good habits that supported my success in other areas of life. But under the surface, fear still ruled. The fear of being judged. The fear of being seen and ridiculed. The fear of being unlovable if my body didn't match the ideal.

Even now, after all this work, I still haven't thoroughly shaken that fear. There's a voice that whispers when I gain weight:

*What will they think? Will they still respect me? Will they look down on me?*

And the painful truth is: some do. Our culture permits people to be cruel to anyone who doesn't fit the mold. They project their insecurities onto others and call it "concern" or "standards." But I've realized their judgements are not mine to carry. Their opinions say more about them than they ever could about me. A healthy mind is aware—not obsessed with control or perfection but grounded in loving kindness. It's a mind that can look at a soft belly, or a tired body, or a scarred heart, and say:

*Thank you. You've carried me this far.*

It's no surprise that when my body started to change during pregnancy, all those old fears came roaring back. I didn't feel in control anymore. I didn't feel beautiful. I didn't feel like myself. And then came menopause—a whole new wave of body changes, mood swings, and the disorientation of aging. Whoa. Navigating that is no joke. But through it all—pregnancy, motherhood, menopause—I've come to understand something I didn't know when I was a little girl hiding in her own skin:

*My greatest job in this lifetime is to become the greatest friend to myself. To go within. To forgive my misgivings.*

I want to love myself for who I am and who I am becoming. No one taught me how to do that as a child. I was surrounded by adults who, through their own pain, relayed a message to me that I was unlovable unless I performed or conformed. I've been unlearning that message for quite some time, and it's hard. Some days, brutally so.

But I'm an adult now. And I have tools. And I have truth. I was never unlovable. I was deeply sensitive in a world that didn't know how to hold that. And now, I do.

## III. When the Light Came In

I thought that when I finally left elementary and middle school alive, stopped crying in silence, and started feeling good in my skin, my life's trajectory would take a different direction. And in many ways, it did.

I learned better coping mechanisms. I met friends who loved me, saw me, supported me, and let me help them, too. I began to believe in my own potential. I started to dream bigger. Laugh louder. Breathe deeper. And for the first time, I felt like maybe I belonged. Even more miraculously, my relationship with my mother changed.

After the heat of my rebellious years passed, we returned together—not just as mother and daughter, but as friends. She softened. I softened. And in that softness, we found each other again. She got excited for me—my career, dreams, and hopes. And I got excited for her joy, freedom, and growth. I relied on her for so much—her presence, insight, and unwavering belief in me. She became a place where my sensitivity was safe in a world that once punished me for being sensitive. She was where I found unconditional love—the kind that asked nothing of me but to show up exactly as I was. And maybe the most profound shift of all—I began to see her not just as my mother but as a beautiful person in her own right. A woman with fears, with hopes, with dreams of her own. I saw her *humanity*. Her *courage*. Her *longing*.

I saw her not as the one who always had the answers but as someone still asking her questions. That's what made her love feel even more real. We were two women learning from each other—holding space for each other's becoming. And that's why losing her hurt the way it did, because it wasn't just the loss of a mother. It was the loss of one of the most beautiful lights I had ever known.

## IV. Grief as a Mirror: When Loss Reveals the Deeper Wound

When my mother died, it shattered something in me. But it also illuminated something I could no longer ignore. Grief stripped everything away—the roles I played, the armour I wore, the excuses I gave. Gone. All that was left was the raw truth:

*A daughter without her mother. A woman forced to face everything she had spent a lifetime outrunning. A girl who still, deep down, believed she was unworthy of love unless she earned it.*

In the quiet after her last breath, I sat by her side, holding her hand like it was an anchor to a world I wasn't ready to let go of. I begged her in my heart not to leave me. And then—without speaking—she did what mothers do best: She gave me permission to let go.

*Let me go*, I felt her spirit say. She was already light. She had returned to the place of peace. But I? I was still clinging to punishment. To the old stories. To the belief that I didn't deserve to heal.

In those first weeks of grief, the surface pain—the heartbreak of missing her—was eclipsed by something more profound and older: a confrontation with the child I had buried long ago. The little girl who still lived inside me, curled up and waiting. Waiting to be forgiven. Waiting to be loved. Waiting to be seen as enough.

Grief, it turns out, is a mirror. And in it, I saw my past as a memory and a map. It showed me all the places I had abandoned myself to survive. All the ways I had punished myself for being human. For being her daughter. For not being able to save her. Maybe if I had done more ...

Maybe if I had been stronger, better, faster ... maybe she'd still be here.

I know now that those thoughts weren't true. They were echoes of old fears, childhood conditioning, and the deep-seated belief that love must be earned through suffering. But when I remembered my mother's final words to me—"Stress will kill you. Have no regrets."—everything shifted.

That was her final gift to me. She wasn't warning me about schedules or pressure or busyness. She told me: Don't let the weight of unworthiness bury you. Don't spend the rest of your life punishing yourself for things you could never control. Let go. Be free. And so began the slow, painful, beautiful process of forgiving the little girl in me. I had punished her long enough. I had silenced her long enough. I had abandoned her long enough.

Now, I would sit beside her. I would hold her hand, like I had held my mother's. And I would say:

*I'm sorry. Please forgive me. Thank you. I love you.*

## V. The Turning Point: Rewiring My Story with Love

This isn't one dramatic moment when everything changes. It's just a quiet afternoon—coffee cooling beside my journal, the ache in my chest humming like it always did, and a choice. A choice to stop rehearsing pain. A choice to stop punishing myself for not knowing better. A choice to forgive the girl, the woman, the soul I've always been.

This moment—writing this piece—is not just a reflection. It is an activation when I finally decide once and for all:

*I forgive myself. For all of it. For what I did. For what I didn't do. For the ways I stayed small. For the ways I let fear win. For the ways I internalized rejection and called it truth.*

This is not a performance. This is a proclamation. And as I type these words, I can feel the magic of neuroscience and spirit intertwining. Because I now understand: each time I choose the habit of self-love over shame, I'm not just feeling better, I'm building new neural pathways—tiny bridges in my brain that say:

*I am safe to be seen. I am worthy of love, precisely as I am. I do not need to suffer to belong.*

Neurons that once fired together in fear and guilt are rewiring through repetition, reflection, and radical grace. And as I want to deepen this journey, something sacred awakens in my body, too. I've been studying yoga and experiencing the beauty of a daily Sadhana practice—a disciplined spiritual path that asks nothing more than presence. I am coming home to my body through movement, breath, and stillness. For so long, I carried shame in these bones. I saw my body as something to fix, control, and critique.

Now, I bow to it. This body carried me through grief. This body danced even when the spirit was low. This body birthed dreams and children. This body survived.

As I fully embody my fifth decade, I honour this vessel—not as a battlefield but as a temple. Through yoga, I fully return to the space I once tried to escape. Through dance, I wake up to life again. And every word I write is meditation guiding me to a beautiful gift. I am no longer just a mind trying to fix the past. I am a woman embodying the present. Every stretch, every breath, every drop of sweat is a prayer:

*Thank you for carrying me this far. I will not be afraid of being abandoned, because I will not abandon you anymore.*

And through it all, I return to my sacred mantra:

*I'm sorry. Please forgive me. Thank you. I love you.*

This is not just healing. This is neuroscience. This is spiritual rebellion. This is Sadhana. This is embodied love.

## VI. Forgiving My Body, My Expectations, and My Becoming

There's one chapter of my life I don't talk about often—maybe because even now, more than twenty years later, the memory still sits in my body like a knot I've never quite unraveled.

In 2002, I got pregnant with my first child. We were so excited; so ready, so full of hope. And then came hyperemesis gravidarum—a brutal, relentless form of pregnancy sickness that brought me to my knees. Nausea so intense I couldn't function. I couldn't eat. I couldn't drive without throwing up. I was dehydrated, dizzy, scared, and confused. My body—a body I had always pushed through discomfort—was suddenly a stranger. A battlefield. And I didn't know how to fix it.

But life didn't pause. I still had responsibilities. I still had to show up to my job. I still had to be Meg.

And so, I did what so many women do—I pushed through. I pretended. I smiled through sickness. I swallowed fear with silence. But inside, I was falling apart.

One day, a friend looked at me—really looked at me—and said, "You need help." She drove me to the hospital. I was severely dehydrated. I needed IV fluids and rest. I ended up staying for a week. I remember lying in that hospital bed, hooked up to tubes, whispering through tears, "I just want to feel well again." But beneath that plea was something deeper: *I don't recognize myself anymore.*

That pregnancy changed my life. It shattered the illusion that I was in control of my body. The moment I created another human being, something shifted—my body was no longer mine in the way it had been. And I never fully came back to it. I thought I would bounce back. I thought I could "do it all." But I was wrong.

And I carried so much shame about that. Motherhood didn't come with the glowing halo I had imagined. I loved and love my children more than myself. I am so grateful that they are healthy, beautiful human beings. But as life changed, parenting came with exhaustion. Insecurity. Overwhelm. Rage that I didn't understand. I missed the life I had worked so hard to accomplish. I held on to a part of me that I didn't want to let go, tired of pretending I wasn't falling apart. Tired of holding the world up while no one held me.

I waited six years to do it again. I prayed that the second time would be easier. But my second child came via C-section—an even worse recovery. My body hurt in new ways. I felt split open in more than just the physical sense. And again, I kept asking, "When do I get to go back to how I was?"

And year after year, I never did. I was so angry about that. Angry that my body changed. Angry that I couldn't control how it all unfolded. Angry that I didn't feel like myself anymore.

Ah, the lessons I've learned. It has taken me years—decades, really—to begin unraveling the bitterness I wrapped around my own experience of motherhood. To understand that the anger was grief, that the shame was inherited. That the voice in my head demanding perfection was never mine.

I'm still recovering—still reclaiming the pieces of myself lost along the way. Still learning how to hold the complexity of being a woman who loves her children and mourns the self she left behind. That's why forgiveness has had to extend all the way back to the moment I first gave life—because in doing so, I also began the long, complicated journey of learning how to give life to myself again. And I don't pass the shame to my beautiful babies.

And so now, through healing practices, writing, yoga, spiritual study, and honest reflection, I offer this blessing to the woman I was:

*I'm sorry. For expecting you to carry more than was ever yours alone. Please forgive me. For judging your body, your fatigue, your rage. Thank you. For the sacrifices. For the softness. For surviving. I love you. Not because you bounced back, but because you kept showing up, even when you were breaking.*

## VII. The Ripple Effect: When Healing Becomes Purpose

For the last fourteen years, I've been navigating this world without my mother—my confidante, my anchor, my soft place to land. Grief has no expiration date.

I still miss her voice, her laughter. The way she could calm the storm inside me with just a look. Nothing felt safe when she left—not even me.

And for a long time, I tried to outrun the ache. I filled my days with doing. Achieving. Proving. I wore achievement like armour, afraid to sit still because the sadness might consume me if I did. Eventually, I reached a place where there was nowhere left to run. The masks stopped working. Everything felt hollow. And my nervous system could not handle fight or flight anymore. Tinnitus—a loud ringing in my head—forced me to be still. What I had been avoiding became the only path forward. I couldn't run from myself anymore. So, I surrendered. To the grief. To the pain. To the reckoning. And in that surrender, I heard a whisper I hadn't allowed myself to believe for years:

*What if everything that came before—the loss, the shame, the heartbreak—was exactly what I needed to experience to step into a life of fully realized purpose?*

That question stopped me cold. It didn't erase the pain, but it transformed the meaning. What if the suffering didn't mean I was broken? What if it was preparing me? Refining me? Calling me into something deeper?

What if the grief cracked me open, not to destroy me, but to help me remember who I came here to be? In the stillness, I realized:

*This is my calling. Not to run from the darkness. But to hold a light for others still finding their way through it.*

That realization was not a single moment—it was a series of awakenings: Publishing my memoir *Butterfly Awakens* and sharing the sacred story of my transformation; becoming a TEDx speaker and saying, out loud, what my younger self never had the courage to—"Wake Up!"; coaching others toward joy, purpose, and flourishing—not from perfection but lived experience; and creating podcasts and conversations that offer people the space to be seen, messy, and whole.

And beneath it all, always, was the heartbeat of forgiveness. The soft hum of Hoʻoponopono.

The daily practice of coming home to myself. The hand over my heart. The breath that says, *I'm still here.*

*I'm sorry. Please forgive me. Thank you. I love you.*

Those four phrases become the architecture of new lived experience. A bridge from the little girl who felt too much to the woman who knows her sensitivity is a superpower. A bridge from grief to grace. From loss to legacy.

## VIII. The Invitation: Come Home to Yourself

If you've made it this far, maybe you recognize some part of yourself in this story—the girl who felt too much, the woman who never felt like enough, or the person still carrying guilt for mistakes made in survival mode. Let me say what I wish someone had told me a long time ago:

*You do not need to earn your way back to wholeness. You are already worthy of forgiveness, because you are human. Being human means we hurt sometimes. It means we fail. It means we grieve, lash out, say the wrong thing, and forget who we are. But it also means we love. We heal. We begin again.*

And today, I'm choosing to begin again—with love. I declare today that I love who I am, and where I am—why not? Why keep punishing myself? It doesn't help me, and it doesn't benefit anyone. In fact, choosing self-love helps me honour the truth that I am human—and humans make mistakes. But humans also grow. And when I know better, I do better. This is my liberation. This is my compassion in action.

This is the invitation I now extend to you:

*Forgive the version of you who didn't know how to love yourself. Let go of the belief that worthiness must be earned.*

And say the words that will change your life if you let them:

*I'm sorry. Please forgive me. Thank you. I love you.*

Say it as many times as it takes. Say it until your inner child looks up and smiles. Say it until you believe it. Say it until you're free. Because you are not broken—you are becoming.

This is the work. This is the healing. This is the homecoming. And it begins right now.

Meg Nocero, Esq., M.A.i.H.S., is a former federal prosecutor turned TEDx speaker, award-winning author, and PhD candidate in Happiness Studies who believes in the art of flourishing and the magic of transformation. She's the host of *Manifesting with Meg: Conversations with Extraordinary People* and the founder of S.H.I.N.E. Networking Inc., a non-profit organization that brings people together to celebrate connection, creativity, and purpose. Through her three books—*The Magical Guide to Bliss*, *Butterfly Awakens*, and *Sparkle & Shine*—Meg inspires others to become more authentic on their path—follow their dreams, embrace joy, and live a life awake and ready to come alive to purpose and meaning.

# THE WIDOW

SANDRA MCQUADE

There was actual dust in her hair. It was stuck into the way she wore it—a French bun is what she called it, or maybe a roll; I'm not quite sure. A very sophisticated name for a twist of hair that perhaps was once a stylish do, now a vehicle for dust bunnies.

The clothes were the same, day after day, after day. And with those same clothes, some type of t-shirt and some kind of pants. There were no showers, no dust removal, no skin scrubbing, no moisturizing, no manicures, pedicures, or toothbrushes. In the daily routine, there was no primping, no preening, and, like I said, no dust removal.

As it got worse, there was the beer truck. The truck showed up—a delivery. What a crazy concept way back then. I think either the first of its kind or somehow a manipulation by her to get what seemed to be the only thing that mattered—the beer. Because beer didn't mind dust or unpedicured rough feet.

The food budget was twenty dollars. Twenty dollars a week. That was supposed to make dinners and lunches, and I guess pay for the beer truck. Who knows? But it sure came up a lot in the yelling—the arguing about the amount, the cost of groceries, and, of course, the impossible task of buying the food, feeding the kids, and paying the Beer Guy. I recall him in the house at times. I'm not sure why. I'll let you figure that out, draw your own conclusions.

Then it got really, really bad. The Money Guy—a tall, good looking, charismatic, non-dust-type—ran the show. Well, he ran the show when he was there, but mostly the Dusty French Roll was alone and trying desperately to do the right things, and all the while keep the beer truck coming.

As time passed, the dust grew and the beer truck came and went, and the food didn't seem enough; the neighbours gossiped, and I think a few people tried to "help." But Dusty French Roll finally snapped. At least that was what Brogue Shoes told the doctor, and who would you believe? Would you believe that shiny Brogue Shoes could possibly have been responsible for sending Dusty French Roll to her quite accomplished nervous breakdown, or perhaps because of the beer, and the mental state, and the day after day of twenty dollars a week for groceries, and with nonexistent battle tools, Dusty French Roll just had nothing left to give and finally snapped?

I'm guessing, since there are always two sides to every story—and I for the most part was only told one—that somewhere in the middle of all of this is the truth. There are a few facts, as there often are with any person who caves, bends, snaps—that at the time of the folding in two, they just didn't have the armour or the weapons needed to survive. So many weapons can help in times like these—you don't need them all, but you need the key ones that can save you. For example, Dusty French Roll was run over by people who were likely more intelligent than her and knew how to get what they wanted. She was also dealing with an alcohol addiction, and I'm guessing there were some pills involved, because I'm pretty sure the good doctor medicated rather than took the action needed to help. Again, this is my guess. Brogue Shoes held a lot of cards—the money, the car, the mistress with the fancy cottage, the skills of a narcissist—and no way was Dusty French Roll prepared for any of that.

So, this brings us to the mental health ward—oh, what fun! A place with many, many cots, and very high ceilings. Brogue Shoes visited there, and although Dusty French Roll was there, her dusty French bun was gone—lost in the war. Shock treatments in those days made you bald. Au revoir, dusty French bun.

In the meantime, Brogue Shoes visited Au Revoir Dusty French Roll from time to time and moved his responsibilities in with his family. Now, on the outside this seems courageous—I mean going to visit Au Revoir Dusty French Roll, continuing to work really hard, and maintaining a house to some degree, and doing all kinds of nice things for his mommy—but taking the young ones to visit the mistress' cottage, well, that was just kind of nauseating, even to people who you'd think were way too young to figure it out. The funny part about being taken to do things when you are young—that the adults know is really in poor taste and displaying such things is very bad form—nobody says it out loud, but your body knows it! Your little body says, "Hey, Brogue Shoes is quite a snake in the grass—doing all of this while Au Revoir Dusty French Roll is getting her head blasted with whatever it is that is supposed to make her better." But you know people do what they want and need to do, and I guess, for Brogue Shoes, it was the last bit of joy he had in his life, because he died.

Brogue Shoes—despite all of his charm, charisma, hard work, curly hair, trench coat, and the mistress—got cancer, suffered, and, like watching Dusty French Roll, we watched Brogue Shoes get thin, white, sick, and barely able to colour in a children's colouring book. And he just died.

Well, that truly sucked because Au Revoir Dusty French Roll was still getting blasted in her head, and now Brogue Shoes up and died. Now what?

Somewhere during Brogue Shoes' demise and Au Revoir Dusty French Roll's so-called "treatments", certain people were tasked with caring for certain little ones. So many secrets—so many secrets. Let's just say that Brogue Shoes had a great many secrets within his support system, and not all the secrets were well intended, kind, trustworthy people. And yes, some should never have been allowed around children. I know, for a fact, that some of these people knew that some of the other people should never be around children, but hey, who am I to speak up?

But alas, not all is dark and dreary and horrific. There were the parents of Au Revoir Dusty French Roll—well, one mother and one stepdad, the driver of an 18-wheeler who stepped up to the plate to help as often as possible but also, I'm sure, told to mind his place at times.

That's how the story goes, anyway. But the best memories—the most joy, most totally wonderful love and kindness—came from Au Revoir Dusty French Roll's mother and 18-Wheeler Guy. Between the baldness, the death of Brogue Shoes, and the caregiving by the caregivers who should not have been around children, 18-Wheeler Guy was the most solid and trusting person going. 18-Wheeler Guy brought the first puppy, brought the first budgie, and took the responsibilities to car races and sporting events. 18-Wheeler Guy smelled of musty clothing—the most delicious smell ever.

Special P, aka Pudowa, was likely adopted out of necessity. A search for comfort and safety, this little feather pillow provided all of these needs. Open a musty closet, cozy up to a blanket that hasn't been washed in some time, and there inhale the very essence of Special P. Couple that with the feel of velvet, and soft, cold folds, when touched by little hands—encouraged by imagination—Special P could transport you to places far away from people who shouldn't be looking after children. Special P was the one consistent source of love, strength, and safety. I wonder who Special P really was—likely a guardian angel sent by the Universe, who's smell cleared the responsibilities head, let her inhale comfort and safety, touch softness in a world that was so hard, in living and in being.

Special P lived for a long time in 18-Wheeler Guy's musty hall closet, and when he was gifted, he became the anchor of safety.

Time passes, not that much, but these details as told to me were a little sketchy. Au Revoir Dusty French Roll gets a pass out of the high-ceilinged place with the brain jolting machinery and is now given full throttle access for the care and safety of her charges.

With 18-Wheeler Guy and the mother by her side to support, off we go—at least away from those who should have never looked after children—to far lands on the east coast, where streets are paved with hopes and no one is wearing brogues. 18-Wheeler Guy sets up Au Revoir Dusty French Roll with an apartment, food, some cash, and I recall, a very nice carpet. It was a carpet that was supposed to hang on a wall. We'd never seen such a thing, as carpets were for the floor. But this tapestry of a carpet was sporting the most beautiful deer, and 18-Wheeler Guy wanted us to have it. Having spent much more than he should have already for furnishings, somehow that carpet slipped into a worn leather satchel and got secreted into the back of the car. 18-Wheeler Guy knew how to get what he wanted, and that carpet came to the new digs.

18-Wheeler Guy and Au Revoir Dusty French Roll's mother bid farewell and drove back to the big city, leaving Au Revoir Dusty French Roll and her charges on the east coast—the brogue-less land of sugar and spice and everything nice—and users, and drug addicts, and convicts, and drunks, and more characters that do nothing to help the shaky legs of an addict in recovery, scared out of her mind, unable to cope, once again totally without armour and tools.

This is when Au Revoir Dusty French Roll received her new name. She was called it mostly, I think, behind her back; it wasn't a very nice name at all, and even though its definition was a mystery at the time, the way it was pronounced just made it clear that there was nothing positive in its meaning.

Again, burdened with caregivers and freeloaders who also should never have been around children, the charges of the Widow, aka Au Revoir Dusty French Roll, and Brogue Shoes lived life as if in a real live pinball machine. Getting shoved, jolted here and there, hitting the various pegs, and ultimately tilting.

The Widow, who now had absolutely zero tools, was in the war of her life. No armour, no army, no life, just a dead person walking. A human whose very spark, spirit, and will had been eaten firstly by Brogue Shoes—the first war, the first battles without armour, without tools—and now she just let it all implode; let the wolves in—the kind of broken people that use other broken people, the addicts that are so desperate they take from those who are even worse off than they are. The types of people who have seen it all, who are scavengers, who take for the sake of taking because no matter what they steal, it may get them what they are looking for—money, drugs, booze. And at the bottom of the list of importance, maybe some food.

The Widow was toast, was done, was no longer even able to muster any type of brain power that could even put a square peg into the square space. There was nothing left. The east coast road proved to be even more horrific of a battle zone than the previous horror, and then the brain jolts, and then the beer truck. The swarms of Locusts just came in and began eating up anything that was left, and with that came the Truant Officer.

The Brown School was an old school somewhere up the street from the east coast apartment, where the Vultures and the Locusts frequented—fighting, bleeding, singing Creedence Clearwater Revival songs most nights when the booze was flowing. Where people who should never have been around children visited. The Boxer, however, was different. He provided safety and some hope, and sometimes food, and always a tender hug, a sweet moment. In fact, this Boxer went on to become an advocate for the youth of his area. But the Boxer was a kid himself, and so the CCR tunes continued. And the booze, drugs, abuse, and fear continued.

The Brown School ratted to the Truant Officer, who paid the Widow a visit, and inquired as to why one of hers did not attend school. The Widow, of course, blamed the kid, but it's kind of hard to go to a school that is far up the street, with its high ceilings, when you are needed in the east coast apartment because the Widow is an enormous mess and had to be watched and woken up from various stupors. And someone had to watch the Vulture people and the Locusts because they would have taken the actual furniture right out of the place, or worse—maybe they would have killed the Widow.

The Truant Officer informed Skittle Guy, aka Children's Aid, to come and take the Widow's responsibilities off to dinner to talk about God knows what; the entire time, the little outing just reeked of fish. You can't con the responsibilities of Brogue Shoes and Dusty French Roll because they have been trained in survival and can sniff out a con a hundred miles away. As it happens, the guy who handed out the Skittles turned the wrong way on the highway on the way back and quite literally stole The Widow's responsibilities right out from under her nose. There is nothing nice about getting a clean bed and healthy food when it comes in the form of an orphanage.

After some time had passed, the Widow's mother and 18-Wheeler Guy came and saved the Widow's responsibilities from the orphanage—also a place where people who should never look after children, looked after children. Although there was one kind person, Clicker, who clicked her gum as if her life depended on it; maybe it did.

The Widow, now left without her responsibilities, continued to be a dead person who actually walked. 18-Wheeler Guy returned her responsibilities to visit her for years and years and years. Eventually, one of them, the boy, stopped visiting. Who could blame him? When the new baby came, that was too much to take for him—totally understandable. How is it possible that the Widow brings another life into the world when the other lives she brought here were shattered?

For years and years, the other responsibility waited—waited for the day the Widow somehow found the necessary armour, the army, the tanks—begging her to see a priest, a counsellor, Alcoholics Anonymous (AA), someone, anyone. Twice, the Widow tried to come to the big city and change. Each time, she was returned, along with the new responsibility, back to the land of the Locusts and the Vultures.

I waited for years and years for the Widow to muster whatever it is that broken, defeated, ruined, empty, destroyed people need to muster to become what she wanted to be at the beginning of her marriage and at the birth of her children. As a kid, I watched her disintegrate—rot from the inside out. Mostly alone, because she was so far gone, that even the offer of help was now so far out of reach. There was just no spirit, only a deep and wildly horrific sadness and the anger of a wild beast.

I had one week of my life with her without any alcohol—the week I took my three-month-old son to meet her. That was the one week she gave me her sober self. Au Revoir Dusty French Roll, aka the Widow, held and fed that baby with a softness and a love that I had always dreamed would come my way.

I started forgiving her when I was five years old. When I was standing in the bedroom she shared with Brogue Shoes, I offered her a white-and-green striped shirt and a pair of black pants to wear instead of the dirty clothes she never changed. I forgave her when I tried to brush the dust out of her hair, because I knew that no human being wanted to live a life like that. I knew because her soul told my soul, over and over again, that she wanted to be different, but she never had the armour, the army, or the tools to fight. I forgave her, over and over again, with every one of my own failings, my shortcomings, my own humanness. Nobody chooses to walk in a living world when you are already dead.

Au Revoir Dusty French Roll, aka the Widow, taught me everything about trust, pain, hopes, love, courage, joy, and—most importantly—forgiveness. Joan passed away in hospital due to a tumour on her heart. Can you think of anything more poetic? All three of her children were at her side.

Sandra McQuade is a visual artist based in Ajax, Ontario, and an Artist and Certified Coach with Awakening to Harmonious Integration (ATHI). She is also a certified yoga teacher, having earned her designation in Nicaragua. Actively involved in several art organizations, her juried paintings have received recognition and awards. New to storytelling, Sandra is honoured to contribute *The Widow* to this collection, offering a narrative shaped by lived experience, reflection, and forgiveness.

# KṢAMĀ PEAK

DR. ERIN MANTIS

*August 10, 1994*

I have no memory of the impact; no sound or image comes to mind. It is as if that moment in time never existed. When I came to, I remember feeling sheer raw panic. It was like an internal alarm unleashing adrenaline as I was catapulted into flight. I recall being panicked, thinking, "What have I done to myself? To Michelle?"

I had crawled out of the car, escaping onto the pavement baking in the summer heat. Someone was trying to help me. I looked down, feeling and seeing the parts of my body that were swelling. "Get the shoe off," I was screaming in my head as the sandal tightened around my ballooning ankle. I became aware of blood oozing from my elbow, a bone piercing through the skin. I looked away and saw that Michelle was still in the car. She appeared to be paralyzed, crying silently and not moving.

I heard the sirens. That piercing noise was the last thing I heard before I crashed into another dimension, one that would rupture the narrative I had been living, delivering a jarring, painfully visceral awakening that has stayed with me to this day.

## Finding Kṣamā: The Journey Begins

As the ground shifted beneath my feet, I felt a weight like a stone tightening deep in my chest. Twenty feet away, a jagged fissure appeared and would soon reach where I was standing. I was going to have to ascend quickly. My body spoke. I leapt toward the rocky outcrop and grasped the edge with both hands. I could feel the sting of the rocks lace into my palms. I struggled to find my footing but managed to boost my body up onto the ledge above my head. I tried to calm myself, took a deep, slow inhale, and realized there was no going back ...

The pause is brief, and I seem to have taken it for granted. The mountain floor heaves again, and before I can catch my bearings, I feel my body falling. I know I should be terrified but instead I felt a need to surrender as I fell into a crimson canyon ...

*August 12, 1994*

I woke with a start, catching my breath to realize I was not falling but lying in a hospital bed, in excruciating pain. I looked to my right, and Michelle, my boyfriend's sweet younger sister, lay in the hospital bed beside me. She and I were good friends, and now hospital mates. Over the next little while, we would briefly chat with each other in the moments when we were somewhat lucid and not surrounded by family members. It felt comforting to be with her, though I couldn't help feeling terrible that she had been with me when the accident happened.

Fortunately, it turned out I was not at fault for the crash. I think I did the best I could to avoid swift decapitation and having the blood of others on my hands. It was either: slide under a transport, shift lanes into oncoming traffic, or slam right into a steam roller smack dab in the middle of a busy highway (why would someone think that parking a steam roller on a busy highway was okay?). I chose the steamroller—and the steamroller has shown who had won. Definitely not the two young women in the Acura Integra. All this thinking is making me tired. Heaviness falls over my eyes. I am once again falling into the dream state, as if time had never stopped.

## The Crimson Canyon

I landed on what felt like a trampoline, cradled in a warm embrace. As I was gently lowered onto the floor of the canyon, faceless shadows of bodies escaped into the crimson darkness. It was eerie, and the sense of calm I had felt drained away as they disappeared.

I felt someone's—or something's—eyes on me. A frail figure emerged from the shadows, slowly walking towards me. She reached out and, oddly, I could feel familiarity in the touch of her bony hand as it intertwined with mine. She started to speak, "My dear child, you are in a collective experience of being human. I can feel how overwhelmed you are—and frustrated and concerned—for your path forward. But I know you, and I trust you will figure it out."

"I have known you since you were born, and your path to understanding requires you to know that you are loved and supported. You must reach out to the right people and be accepting of their kindness and security, even if you cannot see or fully understand in the moment."

I was entranced. I just wanted to stay with her; she was so comforting. I lay my head in her lap as she ran her long fingers through my hair—a habitual gesture she had made so many times before. I took a long, deep breath and closed my eyes, feeling at peace. When I woke, she was gone.

I lifted my body off the rock she had been seated on and began exploring the canyon. I found a tunnel that led to a tall stone staircase. After five minutes of walking upwards, I came to an archway of amber stones with a large oaken door.

*August 15, 1994*

The door to the plane was slowly closing, and I felt the tears streaming down my cheeks as I looked out onto the tarmac from my stretcher. I could see my dad standing on the runway with my stepmother. I was in an air ambulance that would fly to Toronto where I could receive the medical interventions I required. I had pleaded with my dad to come with me, to no avail.

They had stabilized me for five days in Thunder Bay to prepare me for the trip. My mom and stepdad had already left for Toronto to support me through the next leg of my healing journey.

My dad had been my hero up until the age of twelve or so. Things happened that would cause my hero to fall. But being loaded into a plane with fear and uncertainty swelling in my throat was one of those defining moments when you need that safe person to be by your side. I vowed, in that moment, that I would never desert my children in their time of need. The stretcher was secured and then the door shut tight. Then, I was out again ...

## The Amber Archway

I pushed the door and it opened onto a pathway of amber stone that led to a suspension bridge. There was mist and rain. I could hear someone sobbing.

I walked to the bridge, and through the gloom perceived the face of a young child with tears falling from her eyes. Her face was scrunched; her lips were quivering. She looked familiar. She looked like a younger version of me.

I gently called to her, “It is okay. You are not alone.”

She responded, “I am lost.”

I asked her, “Where do you live?”

She said, “Thunder Bay.”

“Oh, that is where I grew up, too.”

She paused for a moment. “Oh! Then you can take me home with you, and take care of me.”

“I don’t think I am capable of taking care of anyone right now.”

“Oh, that is too bad,” the little girl said.

“What do you need?” I asked.

“I need to be with people and feel okay with being sad, uncertain, and even happy. I need to know I am going to be okay, and that I can trust you again.”

“That doesn’t seem like too much to ask.”

“Somehow, I was forgotten and left alone with no one to take care of me.”

I told her, “I am sorry. I have not been very present for you for a while now and, as things are, I cannot take care of myself right now.”

I felt inconsolable pain mixed with the warmth of the tears streaming down my face. We were both crying again as I stood on the suspension bridge, feeling the warmth of her tears falling around me. I held my arms open to her as she turned away.

I yelled, “Please come back!” I could feel the suspension

bridge swing back and forth. The little girl came running down the bridge. I lifted her into the air, swung her around, and hugged her close. "Can you forgive me and be patient with me while I adjust to my new reality?"

She looked into my eyes, gently pushed the wisps of unruly hair behind my ear, and said, "Yes!"

I told her, "I promise I will never leave you again. But I can't promise I'll be perfect at this."

I felt her lean into my body, and her spirit drifted inwards. I sat down on the bridge for a moment. I looked up again and saw a message written in an amber hand:

> *Forgiveness becomes the bridge between us. It connects souls, not because we excuse harm or loss, but because we find salvation in our newfound ability to take care of ourselves with each person we encounter and that keeps us all safe. True forgiveness arises not from neat endings or getting exactly what we think we deserve, but from shared imperfect humanity and the trust we have in ourselves. Holding yourself in the cradle of compassion while holding the other is profound and an act of spiritual contrition and enlightenment.*

*August 16, 1994*

I woke up in Toronto in a hospital bed in the Wellesley hospital—somehow more at rest. My mom was overflowing with relief to see me, broken but alive. In both my career and, very close to my heart, within my family of origin, I know the intimate closeness of being present to the loss of a child.

My mom and my stepdad showed up in every way they could, under every possible auspice, determined to help me find my way through.

My dreams during that time were vivid and relentless, their revelations washing over me with equal parts intensity and relief. They whispered to me that I could finally become the adult in my own life—that perhaps I could even release my father from the responsibility I had carried as his to fulfill.

Sometimes the absence of integrity, when reflected back at you, becomes its own teacher. In a roundabout way, he showed me what it meant to find integrity within myself. I began to wonder: What if I responded to myself the way I would to my own child, as I did in the Amber Garden? I know I would make different choices.

Even in fear, I am capable of being present for myself. And I hold faith that I will find the people who remain—the ones who stay for all the right reasons.

## The Mountainside

I began to feel cold and hungry; I could hear a squeaking sound. As I followed the path, there appeared on my right a short older man, well-muscled with a large auburn beard. His clothes were dirty. He had a dog with him who came running at me, barking to protect his master. The man called to it in a rich Scottish brogue, "Oh Fergie, pull back. She is harmless."

I offered my hand to introduce myself to his cold wet nose. He matched his master's colouring, a Rough Collie with sable markings and a huge white mane. What was a Scottish gentleman and his Collie doing on this mountain? *Seems odd*, I thought to myself.

He lumbered over to me and said, "The mountain offers you what you need. It is up to you to take it."

He paused to let me soak that in and then asked, "Are you okay?"

"Yes. And how did you know that was what I was thinking?"

"Just a feeling," he said as he pulled me up and I dusted myself off. "You look like you need a cup of tea and some biscuits."

"Oh, yes please."

He smiled and asked, "How is your journey so far?"

"Very interesting. Unexpected. Lovely. And a bit scary."

"Yes," he nodded. "Exactly what you need, Lass. That is why you came."

"Yes. I suppose so."

"Follow me."

Fergie excitedly jumped up and down and trotted off behind his master, looking behind to make sure I was following them.

"Um, my name is Erin. What is your name?"

"Angus. Hop in."

It was what looked like an old gondola attached to pulleys and cable lines. I hesitated and he said, "We don't have all day. It is safe. Don't worry, you have made it this far."

I climbed in and the gondola started to rise. We soared past beautiful sunlit ridges, remnants of the golden sun shining through as sundown was upon us. We finally reached his hut, which was a quaint little cottage perched halfway up the mountain. A fire pit was surrounded by large wooden chairs with quilted pillows and blankets.

He invited me into his cottage. I was met with hanging iron pots and pans, patchwork curtains, mismatched teacups and dishes, antique furniture, and an old stove with the smell of thyme, fresh baked bread, and firewood. There was an unmade cot in the corner with a quilt of unique woven fabrics and fluffy pillows.

He offered me hot fragrant tea and steaming scones with

butter, cream, and jelly. I sat down and Fergie lay by my feet, waiting for his scone patiently. I ate quickly and then felt a wave of fatigue wash over me. He said, "Take a lie down on the cot and when you wake, we will have ourselves a warm meal by the fire."

Fergie came in and curled up beside me as I drifted into the sweetest and deepest sleep I could remember. I awoke to the aromas of breakfast being prepared. The golden sun had come up. Angus commented, "You slept through the night, which was good because you have quite a climb in front of you." He pointed to the equipment I'd need for the next stage.

"Come sit." He laid out the fixings and I dug in. He asked, "So what brought you here?"

"I am paralyzed and I am unable to move forward. I cannot let go. I am stuck and I'm drowning; I feel no relief from the pain."

"Oh, I see. That is a very, very tricky one. I am sorry for your pain."

"Thank you," I said, as I quietly looked down at my plate.

"And so, do you have anything going for you?" Angus didn't appear to be shy about cutting to the chase.

"It feels like nothing, because nothing seems to matter at the moment."

"Come on, Lass, have you truly lost everything? The oxygen to your breath?"

"Well, you have a point there, Angus. I do have the air in my lungs, hence the life in my body and the spirit in my soul at present, and that might be enough to carry me through."

"Sometimes we have just enough hope and breath to get us out of the hole and over the hump to get back to a time in our life when we felt we had more than what we needed to thrive."

"I don't know if or how I am going to walk again or live without pain or find my way back to a normal life."

"Well, I am going to lay it to you straight: *Do not give up your passion and purpose—your reason for being here—in exchange for resentments and a commitment to a life of nothingness, and what seems like a solid case of victimhood. You will either lead from the first transgression to the next and so on and so forth, or your life can be something special—one full of creative pursuits, passion, resilience, forgiveness, and love. This, coupled with the practice of compassionate unburdening over and over again because, to be honest, it won't always go the way you think it should."*

"Oh, well. Thank you for your brutal honesty."

"Well, is anyone else giving it to you straight up?"

"No, not really. People mostly feel sympathy, compassion, or pity right now."

He said, "Listen, the hurts will rise and fall like the tide, and you have the choice to drown in them continuously or to be freed because you have consciously stayed present and actively released them. The losses set you free; not from the pain, but from the entrapments of resentment allowing you to enhance your dreamer's mind."

I just sat there, soaking in his wisdom.

"I've come to believe in my own humble life experience that forgiveness is not a final destination. It is a practice. A posture. A quiet vow we make again and again, especially in the small moments of the sacred pauses before reacting—the breath before judging, the grace we give ourselves when we fall short, and the compassion we extend, when our hearts can feel heavy. Some chapters are long and some are short; some impenetrable and some make sense like a homecoming. The point is to find yourself in each one."

I leaned over and hugged him, whether he wanted me to or not. "What about you, Angus?"

"Oh no, this is about you. Let's get you on your way; you are not there yet."

"Thank you, Angus. You are a wise soul and hospitable host."

I leaned down to pet Fergie for the final time. "Be good Fergie and take care of Angus." I walked away thinking maybe I will have a Fergie in my future.

I am on my own again, feeling teary at leaving them. I clipped into my gear and started pulling myself from one ledge or crag to another—once again, talking to myself. About twenty-five feet up from Angus' ledge, I can no longer see them as I look down. I can see the jutting edge I must reach that Angus showed me on a map, above.

I thought to myself, *It is true action time. I am ready to push into the discipline I need to keep up with this journey. This is where I have to dig deep for confidence, determination, and steadfast ways to keep going. This is going to take every bit of strength I can muster,* as I peered up the side of the mountain.

I heard myself saying, "Are you willing to push harder, and work through the pain of the challenges ahead of you?" I peered downward and saw a weaker version of myself, hanging by a thread. The self-doubt is creeping in; she is waning and calling to me. "Let's stop, give up," she whispers. For a moment, I wavered. "Let's skip the hard part, but what would that mean?"

I recognized this was another starting point. I pondered—could my life have been a slow crash in motion leading to this moment, or was my life a series of moments meant to be cherished regardless of this moment? Is this the defining time or was it my whole life?

Maybe everyone's life has those punctuating moments that deliver them from one reality to another—forcing them to look in the mirror and change or commit to a life of mediocrity and denial mixed with acute moments of sadness. I can say that I am not willing to take the latter path; if I don't get through this, the mountain can take me.

Looking down, I felt a strength inside me firmly assert my fearful and apathetic self. "I need you to buck up and find your strength because we have to be together on this."

"Okay, okay," the whispering, apathetic one responds, as she slowly floats up and is enveloped by my body, increasing my strength.

My muscles tighten and are burning, and my mind is laser focused. "I feel like the queen of this mountain; I will embody the one I am becoming. Maybe I am not the queen, but a tigress. Okay, now I am just laughing at myself."

My final push put me over a ledge. I stood up and looked out over expansive green floating meadows with flowers and, in the middle, a gigantic Heart Fire tree—something I had only read about. Only, this one had no blooms.

*September 3, 1994*

After multiple procedures, surgery, disappointments, and a series of problems to overcome, I finally left the hospital with the window facing the large weeping willow on the greenery out front, in a somewhat put back together state of being. Only, I felt I had been put together differently from my configuration of the previous me. I was facing a number of surgeries ahead, a loss of independence, and the knowledge that I would never be fully functioning or as pain free as I was pre-accident. I was on a new life course—one I would not have chosen but had no choice but to accept.

The year following the accident, I had strep throat four times. My immune system was compromised, I could barely walk, and I needed to sleep a lot; I did try to nap outside of our house among the trees in our backyard in the country to make the atmosphere more inviting, much like the dreams.

## The Heart Fire Tree

I pulled myself up fully and started running through the meadows. I had the sensation of floating from one meadow to the next in an attempt to reach the Heart Fire tree. I felt the soft breeze in my face and a magnetic pull that was reminiscent of when I would feel the safety of my dad coming home from work or a trip and I knew I was going to see him, and then relief would settle in.

As I got closer, I saw the outline of a figure standing with his back toward me, under the tree. As if he could hear my footsteps, the being turned around to face me. I thought my heart was going to leap out of my chest. I ran faster and I jumped into his strong arms. I buried my face in his neck, breathing him in and I said, "I found you!" He held me up close to his face and our eyes locked, brimming with excitement.

He said, "My current self knows I have to wait for our future together. I miss you without even knowing you accept in my heart that has an intuition about our future."

As our lips gently touched, I felt my body relax into his; there was nowhere else I wanted to be but in this moment. It felt like forever. It was the oddest thing; I did not recognize him, but I felt I had known him forever.

He said, "Come here, I have something for you."

He slowly knelt down before me and peered up. I looked down into his earnest face. "I am asking for your hand in our future together, with our kids and all the chaos that comes with a family that stays together, through any storm, united." He took my hand and was about to slip an emerald ring on my finger when he asked, "Will you promise me that you are committing to live a full, crazy, beautiful life that will be a great love story because we are meant to be together? Will you open your heart to everything that this one life will offer you in weird and unusual ways? Your story is not over, and neither is mine through us. I will be with you in spirit every step of the way. I know, together, we will both be better versions of ourselves. I will patiently wait for you to join me. I promise you I will not go anywhere until we find each other. Do not hold back from living wildly and greatly in every possible way until we meet, and from then on. Now you must go."

"I can't leave you. I won't leave you. I cannot do this next bit on my own."

"You must because it will make you who you need to be for us to meet and be stronger together. You cannot give up. You have no choice or you will live in grief and misery, and we will not meet in the middle. Our paths will not cross if you do not pursue your dreams that will bring you to us! I am here to support you the same way I will in our future together. You can do this. You will conquer what lies ahead."

"I will never leave you in my heart or my soul."

"You don't have to," he said, "but you have to come back to yourself first, and then to us."

"I promise, I have already begun that journey back."

He placed the ring slowly on my finger, pulled my body in tightly for a final goodbye, his lips lingering, and then he was gone. I looked up at the greenery of the huge Heart Fire tree and there was a swirl of blossoming rose- and emerald-coloured flowers in front of my eyes. It was the most beautiful thing I had ever seen. The wind calmed and the air stilled as the meadows quieted. I felt his presence to guide me, and I moved on.

There was a tunnel carved into the mountain at the edge of the meadow. As I approached the opening, I beheld a message carved into the stone, written in a brilliant shade of blue:

*Reckoning is the soul's pause, where we allow the seeping in, what we push so hard against.*

*We are here not to punish, but to witness, where truth can no longer hide, where pain is named aloud, and the burden we carry is either claimed...or released.*

*This is where we truly surrender, until we are done to reclaim our soul again.*

The goosebumps popped up all over my arms as I heard the strong winds whistling through the tunnel, with voices summoning me to enter. I was frightened but undaunted. I pulled my jacket closer around me as I cautiously entered. The wind was strong, and I had to lean hard into it.

*September 1994 to August 1997*

Healing in the aftermath of the surgeries, dealing with the pain and the unknowns, and yet needing to accept my fate physically was an adjustment. I focused on the messages the suitor in my dream gave me, and I trusted that I would find love and loyalty in my future—not because he said it would be so, but because I trusted I would grow enough for it to be so.

There was also a change within my family; another divorce and the invitation of a new family through my father's choices. I was in university and he was starting over with toddlers and babies. The upside in this change in circumstances was the addition of three amazing brothers. At the time, I felt I could lean into my current life with my supportive boyfriend, friends, and family who were present and whom I cared deeply about, alongside the education I was pursuing in psychology. I was moving forward and forging my own life with a strong pulse and soft hum coming from my own voice that I was using more and more.

## Finding Ksama

The tunnel walls pulsed with a soft hum, not from others, but from within. Each echo sounded like my own voice—layered and distorted—as though different parts of me were taking turns to be heard.

One voice whispered sharply: "They will never accept you. It does not matter what you do."

Another one, weary and familiar, sighed: "You must submit. Rejection lies at the other end of that decision."

The voice of guilt always weighs in: "I feel guilty if I don't do this ..."

Then, pure fatigue of the uphill climb, the overwhelm: "I just need to sleep; this is so much, I don't know if I can do this ... I am scared ..."

And then, the harder and more insistent, barked: "Keep pushing, keep fixing, keep proving. If you stop, you will fall apart."

I slowed my steps, pressing my palms against the damp stone. The echoes vibrated through me, rising and falling, each voice trying to pull me back into the shadows of who I had been. Somewhere beneath their noise, faint but steady, another voice emerged. It was quieter, but unwavering; the one I was becoming and my younger self needed me to be: "You are still here. You are evolving at the right time and pace. Keep gently but firmly moving forward, because you know what you need to do; you can trust yourself."

I took a breath, leaned into that sound, and with each step, the echoes of doubt began to fade—though, I knew they would try to return. The tunnel was not just a passage; it was the landscape of my own mind. Only I could choose which voice to follow.

And with that, the air fell quiet with no motion or sounds. I ran to the end of the tunnel, leaving the voices of my past behind and hanging on to the future. I reached the open air and kneeled on the ground. I took a long inhale and breathed it out. I felt the unburdening of that stone in my chest.

The tunnel opened up onto another level of luminous glassy rock. I followed a path that led to a calm pool. I peered into the pool and saw my reflection. "Oh! I appeared more grounded or confident in this next step, hmm. I think I will be okay."

The water was a refreshing cool temperature as my fingers dragged slowly across the surface, making a ripple that altered the reflection. I pulled back quickly as I felt a burning sensation in my fingers. The reflection had shifted.

I had aged, but time had not been kind to me. I paused. I know I still have time; it is clear I can influence my life's trajectory.

From beneath the water, my little girl from the Amber Garden reappeared, smiling at me. "I know; I know I see you, I feel you. I am here, and I will not let you down." She playfully dove under the water, and I dove in after her. I swam quickly towards her, it felt so refreshing; she let me catch up, I hugged her one last time.

*I will play big and play free, no longer trapped ...*

I commit to this feeling and this experience, as an act of maturity and evolution that I cannot deny. I can see and feel myself holding my Amber Garden girl in a loving embrace, full of surrender and humility, with a strong voice and a loving eye. Can I do the same for those in my life who are human like me and—just like me—have ten reasons why they got here and did not intend to be selfish or hurtful? I must find a way forward to forgiveness for life's follies. I cannot hold on forever; I must truly forgive and be free, because I am in everyone and everyone is in me. We are universally conscious and connected.

I looked beyond the pool with a view to a transparent spiraling quartz staircase. I dried off, grabbed my gear, and began my ascent. I could not see the top of the stairs due to the low hanging mist. As I ascended, the mist parted and there was the most breathtaking and expansive view at the upper peak of Mount Kṣamā.

I had transcended into a grounded unity that was indescribable other than a feeling of pure joy. I felt love, faith, connection; I felt plugged into a different source. I have felt and observed the war we wage with ourselves that overflows onto other people. It is what I have been living. What strikes me most is not the human brokenness, but the resilience that comes if we are open to it.

*August 10, 2025*

"My story is finished. Thank you, Mount Kṣamā Peak," I found myself uttering as I slowly roused from a most wonderful dream. My husband lay beside asking, "Did you have one of those dreams again?

"Yes. They are ever present to keep reminding me:

We forgive because we want to keep showing up for ourselves and for the ones we love. Because, in the end, time is too precious to spend it shackled in the constraints of resentment. Forgiveness is a choice that begins in the hope that says, 'from this moment forward, you are forgivable—and so am I.'"

And so, we begin again.

## Epilogue

In terms of my physical health, I cannot run, but I can walk—something I never take for granted. I have learned to live with the pain, and I believe it helps me to feel more compassion and empathy as a psychologist and human.

Over the years, I have undergone multiple surgeries—from my face to, finally, a right ankle fusion four years after the accident, just before I moved to Chicago to begin graduate school in Clinical Psychology.

It was there that I met my "Heart Fire Tree" husband.

I believe he is the man from the vision—the one who shows up every day with me. We are imperfectly perfect together, with a steadiness that is irreplaceable. Life has blessed us with three children who are healthy, funny, and the truest reflection of our journey. We also share our home with two Rough Collies—like Fergie—named Tommy Hawk and Beureguard (Bogey for short), named after my husband's childhood Collies, and two Morkies—Samson and Delilah. Samson sadly passed in 2024. These dogs have brought endless laughter, joy, and their fair share of mischief to our family's ruckus.

Of course, there are always going to be hardships, but beneath it all I feel a deep commitment and a steady trust that I can meet whatever comes. I ride shotgun on this life of passion and creativity with the people (family and friends) I love most; that, to me, is the wholeness I seek every day.

Thank you for reading my story. I hope it inspires you on your journey to forgiveness, as we all have a story and we all have our dreams.

Dr. Erin Mantis is a clinical psychologist, Clinical Director at Recovery Counselling Services, and coach and creator of Awakening to Harmonious Integration (ATHI). She shares a life-changing experience that blends psychology and spirituality, guiding readers through a transformative healing journey in a visionary dream sequence on Kṣamā Peak. If you hadn't guessed, Kṣamā (क्षमा) is the Sanskrit word for forgiveness.

# FORGIVING GENERATIONS

## JACQUES V. LEROUX

Grampa Joe was a mean, short-tempered old man. I was the youngest of three brothers—Bernie was the oldest, followed by Stephan—and in kindergarten at the time, so I was too young to understand why my grandfather Olivier—or Grampa Joe, as he preferred to be called—was to be feared.

As a young boy, it seemed my family never lived anywhere long enough to put down roots. For a time, we lived in Athens, Ontario, where Grampa Joe lived with his second wife Dona, along with their sons Mike and Mark. From his first marriage, Joe had four daughters and one son, my father Jack—the youngest child, who was born in 1935. Jack moved our family to Athens, where he cut hair with Grampa Joe in a two-chair barbershop on Main Street. Another daughter, Marie, also lived in Athens with her husband Max and their son Jim.

Joe's first wife died before he served as a soldier in World War II. Photos of Grampa Joe in combat fatigues and in his officer's uniform stood proudly on the mantel. This is one of only a few memories I retain from the early 1960s of the inside Joe and Dona's house in Athens.

When Joe went off to fight in World War II, my father and my aunt Juliette were sent to live in one of the many government-funded residential schools run by churches of various denominations. The only memory of life at the convent my father ever shared with us was that Juliette tried her best to protect him whenever the bad people came. We deduced that my father had been subjected to abuse while at the school, where he lived from age seven until twelve.

What we had been cautioned about soon became evident—Grampa Joe did have a short fuse. He had an intensity about him that resulted in frequent eruptions of anger, and I saw him berate Dona and my dad on more than one occasion. I learned from my cousin Jim and step-uncle Mike (who was the same age as me) that it was best just to avoid him, especially when he was drinking. I came to learn that Joe had been affected greatly by having served in World War II and used alcohol to cope with his emotional trauma. Maybe, too, by a secret he kept. He kept private that his first wife was half Indigenous and his mother was full-blooded Indigenous. Joe's father, a Frenchman named Louis, somehow kept his wife's ethnicity hidden—I suppose because of society's intolerance of interracial marriages in the late 1800s. I didn't learn that my grandmother was Indigenous until I was an adult.

When he wasn't cutting hair at the barber shop on Main Street, Joe would spend endless hours in his garage workshop. He was a skilled shipwright who took great pride in handcrafting sailboats. Grampa Joe once gave me a tour of the workshop and showed me the sailboat he was building. I remember this being the first and only time I ever was alone with Joe. I felt trepidation in the moment, fearful he would suddenly turn mean. But Grampa Joe was nice to me during those few minutes. I was awestruck at how he could actually create what I was looking at—a twenty-five- or thirty-foot-long sleek, wooden sailboat. I believe he appreciated my interest and enthusiasm for his craftsmanship; it created a feeling of warmth between us. From then on, I cannot recall that he was ever mean to me. But I was never again lucky enough to visit him in his workshop.

The eighteen months that we lived in Athens was a happy time for me. I learned to swim that first summer, using my father's wetsuit boots tucked in my shorts as flotation devices. Hours a day for a week, I frolicked with my brothers jumping off the Charleston Lake dock by Kelsey's Marina. One day, Jack* tossed me off the dock without my flotation boots. I remember being very frightened of drowning and seeing millions of bubbles rushing past my head. My instincts took over, I started kicking and moving my arms. Pleasantly surprised, I could swim without the aid of the sponge rubber boots. Jack understood that his diving boots, now saturated, were weighing me down more than keeping me afloat.

My brothers and I played a game where Bernie would hold my ankles and Stephan my wrists, and they would swing me three times and toss me high in the air, off the dock, into the water. I loved it, until perhaps the fifth time. We were about to play "baby-brother-toss," and on swing number one a stranger yelled out, "Stop, wait!" my brothers halted on mid-swing number two. We looked where the long-haired, bearded man sitting dockside was pointing. Bobbing on the surface, right where I was about to be tossed was the largest snapping turtle any of us had ever seen. A majestic prehistoric looking beast, easily three feet across and a hundred pounds, with a head bigger than my own tilted up toward the sky, mouth open wide as if waiting for a meal to be tossed to him. The turtle stayed in place for a minute before swimming off. I began to shake at the thought of being tossed on

* Although he was my biological father, in my mind he is "Jack" rather than "Dad" or "Father."

top of that enormous turtle. Needless to say it took a few minutes for me to calm down. We never played "baby-brother-toss" again.

The remainder of that summer, and much of the next, was spent adventuring around Charleston Lake with Mike. Together, Mike, Cousin Jim, my brothers, and I would hike more than an hour to reach a sheer cliff that was our launch pad into the deep, dark, cold water of the lake. By boat we could ride there in ten minutes, but I recall the lengthy walk from our cottages during the hot summer days of 1968 and 1969, the journey taking us down dirt roads and through wide-open cow pastures and fields of tall grass. Such a long hike, especially for us six-year-olds, with the heat of the midday sun beating down on us, draining our energy. Parched and sweaty, we made the long hike exciting by imagining a farmer might pop out of a gully, shotgun raised to fire a warning shot just above our heads to get rid of us trespassers.

We'd pick up the pace as we entered the cool shade of the forest, aware we had reached the final mile of the journey. I vividly remember the smell of damp earth and rot of the fallen trees, and a hundred thin threads of light streaming down through the branches and leaves to the dark forest floor. Walking through shade, cool perspiration on our necks, the trail narrowing and inclining on the final approach to the cliffs. Anticipation rising with the distinct smell of pine needles and sound of water lapping on the shore, we arrived at the cliffs we called "High Rocks."

The exhilaration, the pure adrenaline of stepping off a fifty-foot-high ledge over the deepest, darkest, and clearest water is unforgettable. The speed of the fall and the loud smack of my feet hitting the surface, and the deep silent plunge down ten or perhaps fifteen feet. A small twinge of fear while clawing my way back to the surface. I wonder what lay waiting in the pitch-dark depths below me. Is my prehistoric friend Snappy the turtle down there, perhaps swimming up to take this six-year-old's leg as a snack?

There was one house in Athens we children were told never to go near. I don't recall who cautioned me, but I was warned of the danger more than once. Something bad happened to Bernie in this house that made him very sad. Many years later, I learned that he had been sexually abused in that house by a stranger. I don't know any details or if the abuser faced consequences, but I do know that it had a life-long impact on Bernie, as he chose to emotionally wall himself off to protect himself, I supposed. To not have to be vulnerable.

Evenings in Athens, family and friends gathered to smoke cigarettes, consume alcohol, and often become loud and argumentative. I don't recall any physical outbursts, just plenty of derogatory remarks and blaming and shaming as intoxication levels elevated. Alcoholism was common in our family, affecting Grampa Joe, my father, and his sister Marie. One family get-together at our apartment turned nasty—almost violent. Everyone left abruptly, likely kicked out by my father. I was lying on the couch, pretending to sleep. Jack verbally abused my mother, Mary, for what seemed like an eternity. I felt horrible—really scared—but I didn't want them to know I was awake. I just kept pretending to sleep. I had just turned six years old, and remember this being the fifth home we lived in.

My parents' behaviour continued like this over the years—Jack and Mary engaging in social drinking with friends, the night often ending in a quarrel. Yelling and drinking seemed to happen more frequently, and Jack's outbursts became more extreme, like Grampa Joe's. When we moved to a suburb of North Bay called Nipissing Junction, my brothers and I began feeling the effects of his abusive and toxic behaviour.

In Nipissing Junction, the seventh home I'd known was one of ten houses built on either side of Highway 11, about nine kilometres south of North Bay. Surrounded by forest and a few small lakes, and with train tracks cutting a trail through the woods, it was the perfect setting for young adventurous lads.

Stephan and I became more attuned to nature while living there. We did a lot of camping, hiking, fishing, and wilderness survival. He began trapping rabbits, skinning them to line our leather Ski-Doo mitts, while Mom made stew. We called it *hasenpfeffer* from one of our favourite *Bugs Bunny* episodes. We taught ourselves new ways to fish, trap wild animals, and build a fire from scratch—essential wilderness survival skills. I am certain we could easily have survived an entire year alone out in the woods.

So many skills came naturally to us without any formal teaching. This makes sense now, but we were unaware of our native bloodlines at the time. Likely, Grampa Joe had been conditioned to hide his native heritage. Perhaps he was warned by his father Louis to never discuss it, and so Joe never fully informed his offspring of their true bloodline. As far as we knew, we were pure-blooded French on my father's side.

A favourite memory of when I was eight is Stephan and I jumping on our bicycles Friday after school (I was in grade one), camping gear on our backs, riding a few miles up the dirt road beyond the DuPont chemical plant to Cooper's Lake. We'd pitch our tent, pull out our fishing rods, and hook a few catfish, then clean and cook them in butter on a cast-iron skillet. We did this over a fire we made by hand, carving a foot-long V-shaped channel in a dried piece of hardwood, rubbing long and hard in the "V" with a pointed stick until the splinters began smouldering and eventually became hot enough to ignite when blown on.

We'd spend entire weekends out there, gorging ourselves on catfish, swimming in Cooper's Lake, carving things with our knives, and just being two young boys in the woods, entirely attuned to nature. We'd ride back to our house late Sunday afternoon around sunset, looking like a couple of feral animals. For a time, Mom would ask where we had been all weekend. It seemed normal to us that twelve-year-old and eight-year-old brothers had been fending for ourselves out in the woods for the past fifty hours without informing our parents. Perhaps Mom was okay with our absence because it meant we avoided Jack's drunken and abusive behaviour.

When I was ten, my parents bought a house in North Bay. How amazing it felt! We were finally going to settle down in our own house! And maybe my recurring nightmares would stop. I experienced the same dream once or twice every week: our family is at a party and, for no particular reason, Jack sends me home. I walk in the dark alone for an eternity, only to arrive at the door of our previous house. The door is locked. I knock and discover the house is occupied by another family—we no longer live here. Yikes! Then I awake.

I was sad to leave the wilderness of Nipissing Junction. We had lived in a city before—Toronto—before we settled in Athens. I remember Bernie taking Steph and I for a subway ride on opening day of the Bloor Line. It was free that first day and I recall sitting at the front of the train, fascinated by the speed, mesmerized by the lights flying by in the tunnel. A few weeks later, there was another subway adventure that involved me being trapped under a sidewalk air vent grate by my brothers. I was three at the time. At nearby Lansdowne Station, people would fumble for coins for the fare and often drop change down the air vent by the sidewalk. One day we discovered the trap door on the sidewalk grate was unlocked, so I went down the ladder to fill my pockets. As I climbed up the ladder, Bernie and Stephan closed the grate door and stood on it as a joke. Though they let me out after only a minute, I had a hard time seeing the humour, so I didn't divvy up any coins with them.

North Bay is where my mother grew up, and she still had family and friends there. Mother was a positive influence in my life. She would often tell me I could do anything I set my mind to. My brothers and I earned a weekly allowance of five dollars for completing daily chores assigned to us. We learned about responsibilities, the consequences of shirking them, and the value of earning a dollar. These were important life skills.

Mother favoured Bernie, perhaps due to the abuse he incurred a few years previous in Athens. Bernie developed a deeper connection with Mother, perhaps seeking security of an emotionally stable parent figure. Steph and I were more self-sufficient. Our love of nature was now invested in other things like music and sports. Bernie took an interest in girls, the arts, and expanding his circle of friends.

Bernie also took an interest in religion and became an altar boy. He also developed a love for the theatre and joined a youth community theatre production. Stage performance served as a launch pad for Bernie to explore creative expression, which bore him fruit. On stage, Bernie could wear the mask of an alternate persona. This new-found freedom of expression guided him to a life-long career path in creative arts of various mediums.

Around 1972 or 1973, Jack rented retail space on Algonquin Avenue in North Bay and opened a hairstyling salon that quickly gained popularity and became a commercial success. It wasn't long before he rented the space next door and tasked my brothers and me with helping him renovate to expand his salon. I found it interesting at age eleven to gain practical experience installing plumbing, drywall, painting, and electrical wiring. I was happy working alongside my brothers, with Father issuing directions.

Once the renos were complete, we tore down the common wall between the stores. This was one of the only times we four clicked together with a collective pride of ownership, all contributing to the expansion of our father's shop—JBL Hairden.

Jack loved the spotlight and revelled in the shop's success. But success brought responsibility: rent, payroll, and bills to pay. The romance of operating his own shop faded. Jack didn't have the emotional tools to cope with structure or the stress of success. He drank more, which increased his emotional volatility.

My brothers and I bore the brunt as he went ever deeper into a dark place.

A nightly bedtime ritual for us was to attempt to sneak past our father while he sat in front of the TV, drinking. To get upstairs, we had to make our way through the living room where he would invariably hold one of us captive to retell his life stories. This digressed into verbal abuse of an hour or longer, often lasting until one or two in the morning as he drank and smoked a pipe and cigarettes. I don't remember all he said, but I remember how badly I felt after being degraded and belittled, like I was not a valued member of the family and not even a worthy member of humanity in general. With no defence mechanism, I was confused and emotionally twisted by his behaviour. At twelve years old, I began medicating with alcohol and marijuana.

This unconscionable nightly routine continued for about three years. It paused briefly when Jack began a program of self-improvement. Somewhat remarkably, he came across transcendental meditation and decided the entire family was going to take it up. So, we went to an initiation ceremony and learned how to meditate. All five of us meditated before breakfast and dinner for nearly a year. I really loved it and began experiencing the benefits quickly, finding it similar to the calmness I experienced in nature. Venturing within gave me the same serenity as a wilderness hike—ability to focus more, be calm, and dampen the noise generated by the chaos happening around me. Chaos caused by Jack's alcoholism and verbal abuse, and chaos caused by competing with my brothers for his validation for our achievements, our talents, our efforts. I also continued to use alcohol and marijuana.

Meditation brought our family closer together, but only for a short time. Bernie graduated high school and moved to Toronto to attend the Ontario College of Art. Stephan set out on the road, playing drums in a touring band. Still in middle school, I studied piano and developed skills for high jumping and volleyball. Music was my emotional outlet, enabling me to be a "legend in my own mind"—a mask I could wear to hide my true identity. Pretending to be vulnerable while I emoted in alignment with the song. Early days of imposter syndrome? Echoes of previous generations, perhaps?

Jack made a conscious attempt to live a healthier life. During my first year of high school, we would go for a 5:00 a.m. jog and meditate with my mother around 6:00 a.m. (in the same living room my father had often stripped my self-worth away). After breakfast, I would ride my bike six kilometres to high school for the 8:00 a.m. volleyball practice. Jack would head off to work early to open the shop. This new routine seemed to have a positive impact on his demeanour; however, his attempt at a healthier lifestyle was short-lived. He soon fell back into his habit of over medicating until very late at night and verbally abusing my mother and me.

I was halfway through grade nine when Jack left my mother for a much younger woman. They drove off to Florida together, leaving us alone in the North Bay house on Front Street where we had lived the longest yet—nearly four years. Mother soon sold the house out of necessity, and we moved into an apartment on Lakeshore Drive, near my high school. I was fourteen years old, moving into my ninth home.

It was a challenging time for us. My mother was without a husband, and I was without a father figure; although, I didn't feel like it was a big deal because the "father figure" I had experienced was such a negative influence. I began to use considerable amounts of drugs and alcohol to cope with my feelings. I used some kind of mind-altering substance nearly every day through most of my five years in high school.

I moved to Toronto one week after graduation (my eleventh home) and continued to use substances in one form or another daily for the next thirty years, during which time Jack was almost entirely absent from my life. We would visit during the summer—if both of us ended up going on our annual Leroux guys' camping trip—and saw one another for coffee at Christmas at a Tim Hortons. We would exchange gifts out of the trunks of our cars like a drug deal going down in the parking lot. We seldom spoke on the phone.

The catch-ups were a huge disappointment for me. I would fantasize about a father-son connection, looking forward to sharing all the exciting things going on in my life—my success managing restaurants, recording music, performing in bands, dating girls—all things to validate me. Sadly, Jack wouldn't hear anything I said—interrupting me, constantly talking, and never listening. I always left feeling extremely empty and sad. Dominating the conversation was his mask, his shield protecting his vulnerability and true identity. In the 1990s, Jack discovered his Indigenous heritage and soon became obsessed with researching his family tree. I took no interest in this pursuit, assuming his intentions were purely selfish, as was the case historically.

Eventually, I came to accept that Jack would never change, and I shed any hope for a meaningful connection. I stopped trying, but, ironically, Jack asked me to be the executor of his estate, which brought us closer during his final years. I visited him a few times, maintaining no expectation of insightful father-son discussion, and Jack did not disappoint. We spent those evenings in front of the television—Jack smoking his pipe and drinking his wine. He mellowed in his final years; he became a little less aggressive and arrogant. Before entering palliative care, he told me where he wanted his ashes spread. I found the conversation awkward; his delivery was very matter-of-fact and unemotional.

An Indigenous sacred fire burial ceremony was held for Jack outside the north edge of Algonquin Park at our annual camp site. I had the good fortune of being an active participant as the keeper of the sacred fire. It was lit at sunrise by a native elder friend of my father, Mike Gauthier, who was honoured to perform the day's ceremonies. Mike placed sweet grass, sage, and tobacco on a blanket next to the fire. I kept the fire stoked and instructed everyone who stopped by how to pay their respects. The proper method was to take a pinch of tobacco, walk once around the fire, and drop the tobacco into the fire. Then, speak to the fire as though it was Jack's spirit.

At sundown, I stoked the fire one last time. There were thirty of us sitting around it. Using an eagle feather as a speaking totem, the person holding the feather spoke while all others remained silent. We took turns speaking directly to Jack's spirit, after which Mike conducted an Indigenous ceremonial song and dance. My brothers and I buried our father's ashes next to a tree nearby the fire pit. Mike arranged the stones from the fire pit in a circle around the tree, where a photo of Jack paddling a birch bark canoe and wearing his traditional Métis sash hung from the tree a foot above the burial place. This was a very powerful and memorable day to say goodbye to Jack. Mike later registered this spot with the Ministry of Natural Resources as a sacred Indigenous burial ground. The gift Jack gave to me was making me aware of my Indigenous heritage—a part of my family's true identity that had been kept secret for three generations.

Distance and time had separated Jack and me over my entire adult life, which served to ease my emotional pain when grieving his passing. Knowledge of his unstable upbringing, lineage, and potential abuse planted seeds of empathy and compassion in me that eventually enabled my acceptance of his character defects and shortcomings. I began to consider that the fact we moved home so often was either a coping mechanism or a nomadic gene handed down from our Native ancestry. The suffering I endured from him—the verbal abuse, his angry outbursts, narcissistic arrogance, and inability to openly acknowledge pride for my accomplishments—were likely all symptoms of childhood trauma. I do not excuse Jack's behaviour but have come to forgive him, for we all develop emotional coping mechanisms as a form of self-protective conditioning. My father and Bernie were both mask-wearers.

In the late 1990s after eighteen years of managing restaurants in Toronto, I transitioned into a career in web design. A few years down my new career path, I had achieved a moderate level of success employed by a well-known Canadian corporation in the capacity of digital marketing manager. Bernie had also achieved a decent level of success directing television commercials for a production company in the United States. When his work in the U.S. evaporated, Bernie became frustrated by his unsuccessful pursuit for opportunities in Canada. He developed a resentment for my success and began complaining to Mom that he felt I was rubbing his nose in it. From my viewpoint, I was merely expressing joy for my achievements. I had, after all, returned to school to learn a new skill and worked hard to build my career. Perhaps sibling rivalry, competitive conditioning, and my natural tendency to one-up my brothers had me exuding a little more enthusiasm than was appropriate. I could have tempered my joy a little out of respect and sensitivity for Bernie's situation. Regardless, I know this marked a turning point in our relationship, which continued to deteriorate.

When my wife and I announced our engagement, Bernie

invited me out for a drink to celebrate. Entering the patio bar, Bernie directed me to a table occupied by two men. I was confused. He introduced them and we sat down. In short order, I was subjected to a business pitch—a proposal to partner with Bernie and his compatriots who were looking to leverage my position in some way. I remember being shocked by this ambush, disappointed by Bernie's lack of transparency and this attempt at manipulation disguised as a celebration of my pending nuptials. I let the pitch play out as a courtesy for the two strangers and respect for my brother, all while processing the blind-side. As I left the bar, I felt like I did after a camping trip with my dad—disappointed, deflated, and sad.

My relationship with Bernie came to resemble Jack's and mine. For the next twenty-five years, Bernie remained absent from my life except for brief interaction with short and shallow conversations on camping trips or while we were attending funerals, mostly about him. When Mom visited our home in Pickering, we invited Bernie, his wife, and children for dinner in an attempt to bridge the divide. Bernie's behaviour closely resembled that of Jack's and Grampa Joe's—short-tempered, self-important, narcissistic. He frequently shut down his wife's attempts to speak and belittled her. He dominated the conversation, seldom asked questions about us, and when we did speak, it appeared he listened to respond, not to hear, and would jump quickly into telling us a comparable story of his own experiences. He seemed generally uncomfortable when others spoke, usually quick to respond—similar to how Jack and Joe were.

After our mother passed away, Bernie continued to avoid contact—maintaining distance, sending me annual birthday wishes via text. When we did speak, it usually ended with him saying he really missed us and that we must get together soon. I would suggest an available date or two but would never hear back.

On May 4, 2025, Bernie passed away suddenly from a brain aneurysm at the age of sixty-eight.

Attending his funeral and celebrations of life brought me in contact with his family and circle of friends, many of whom I was once close to. Reuniting with old acquaintances and revisiting memories as old as fifty years stirred my emotions. I anticipated feeling deeper over Bernie's passing and assume the time and distance between us diminished my need to grieve deeply. We hadn't been close for nearly thirty years.

Following his death, I frequently checked myself for resentments, anger, frustration, or residual pain from the past. I felt nothing negative other than sadness for the passing of my oldest brother. I came to forgive him for his treatment of me, remembering that much of his conditioning was beyond his control. Bernie learned how to cope, and part of his coping was achieved through avoidance. In a way, I had been grieving the loss of my brother for the past twenty-five years, though, now I am truly sad to lose the possibility of ever restoring our relationship. I suppose I always believed that one day Bernie and I could put the past behind us and return to being true brothers again.

I started using drugs in 1974 at age twelve and continued until 2016—the year after Jack passed away—when I began my journey of recovery from the disease of addiction. I shared my journey of recovery with my mother and took great comfort in her response as she expressed pride and acknowledgment of my progress and encouraged me to continue on my path of recovery. I had used substances to feel better, to dull the pain and cope with emotions that I never learned to navigate. During the years of my active drug use, I became increasingly antisocial, isolating when I was able so I could use more and more often. Throughout the forty-two years of my active use, I harmed many people. I hid my drug use from my wife for years, making up lies about my behaviour, my physical and mental condition. I lost sight of my authentic self and wore a mask to disguise my true identity.

I had suffered from low self-esteem and became conditioned to constantly seek validation and acknowledgement of my value, my worth. I coped through self-centredness, blaming others for my shortcomings, deflecting responsibility for my actions. I became compelled to control conversations, often reacting with defensive outbursts, similar to how Jack, Bernie, and Grampa Joe behaved. I eventually came to forgive myself, for I know I was not a bad person.

In my tenth year of recovery, I am now diligently working to improve myself, to be a better person. I focus more on physical, spiritual, and mental health, to show up more positively, grateful to experience the many gifts of recovery. A large part of my mental health improvement comes from forgiving my father who suffered his own child-hood traumas, and his father Joe who no doubt had PTSD decades before that condition became an official diagnosis. Through learning to forgive them I learned to forgive my brother, and best of all, myself. I have learned to embrace the unique differences in people. To accept others' character defects as I have accepted my own. To not harbour resentment or point blame at the things I once claimed to be a victim of. I now know that most people's behaviour, including my own, is based on personal conditioning fuelled by a combination of love and abundance, balanced with fear and scarcity.

My spiritual wellness stems from years of meditation, a constant connection to a higher power, and the awareness that life experiences contain lessons. My ability to unlock life's lessons is only limited by my level of open mindedness. Today, I accept the conditioning I once embodied as a product of earlier life experiences, and continue to work on improving, evolving, and becoming gentler and kinder to myself and those around me.

Today, I am able to forgive.

Jacques V. (Vince) Leroux is the author of *Mind Travelers Trilogy*, a science fiction adventure that explores time travel, reincarnation, and out-of-body experiences. He is a lifelong musician and multi-instrumentalist, watercolour artist, meditation practitioner of over fifty years, and an addict in recovery, actively supporting men in their journey of recovery and battle against the disease of addiction for the past decade. Vince resides in a suburb of Toronto with his wife Tracy and their two spoiled dogs, Reuben and Fergus.

# ANOTHER CRACK IN THE ARMOUR

ADAM KUNDER

I still remember that summer night. The kind where the air smells like fresh-cut grass and sunscreen your parents painted you white with. I must've been five years old, playing little league baseball. The dirt diamond felt bigger than life and the sun was still hanging high in the sky. Kids scattered across the field, shouting and laughing in their matching uniforms. Coaches and parents cheering and yelling. Looking back, it was as picturesque as it gets. A perfect summer night.

And then, out of the corner of my eye, I spotted something. A big, beautiful, shiny, red truck. A fire truck. The sun shimmering off it, lights flickering, pulling up and parking right beside the baseball diamond.

One of my best friends' dads was a firefighter. The firefighters showed up from time to time while on shift to support us. Siren off, but red-and-blue lights flashing.

We all ran over. Real-life heroes, standing right in front of us. Real men. Big, strong firefighters. The kind I'd seen in movies. Who ran toward the danger. Who saved people's lives. The kind

I'd pretended to be since I could remember. When they pulled up that day, that was it. That was the moment.

That was when I knew—I wanted to be just like them.

Not only because of the truck, or the gear, or the lights, or the big toys, though that definitely helped. It was the way people looked at them. The way *I* looked at them. With respect. With admiration. With something that looked a lot like love. These men and women were heroes. They mattered. And maybe, if I became one of them, I would matter, too.

Even as a kid, before I could name it, like many, I had a yearning—a wanting to be seen. To be chosen. To be enough.

When you're young and unsure of your place in the world, admiration looks and feels a lot like love. And I thought maybe, just maybe, if I wore that suit, climbed into the truck, and became the one running toward the danger, they'd have to see me. How could they not?

Something I didn't learn until much later, though, is that admiration and love are two very different things.

When I look back now, I know the dream was still real. It still is real. I believe my purpose has always been to serve. To protect. To help people make it out of the dark.

But underneath all of that was something else. Something I didn't have words for back then. I wanted to become the man I didn't always have growing up. The one who showed up. Who inspired. Who stayed. Who chose to learn from their pain and express love anyway.

That little boy at the little league game wasn't just chasing a dream. He was searching for safety. For belonging. To matter. And for someone to see him, the way he saw the world.

And maybe you know what that feels like—wanting to be enough, wanting to be chosen. We all start somewhere, chasing love through performance or seeking safety and worth in approval.

But when the love we receive from the world—from others—is dependent on altering who we are, for the chance to be chosen, we lose the most important love of all: that love we hold for ourselves. That type of love that doesn't ask for you to be anything but who you are, right here. Right now.

The long road ahead would teach me this. It would teach me the importance of forgiveness, not just for others, but for ourselves. And forgiving myself for how long I believed I wasn't, already, enough.

So, I went for the only thing I knew I wanted—the thing that seemed to hold everything I'd been searching for. And just like that, firefighting became the path.

Through the chaos of my own childhood and adolescence—and through divorce, obesity, a bad slide into drugs and alcohol, trouble with the police and at school—that yearning to be seen only grew louder and louder. I didn't know it at the time, but I was using any escape, any pain, as power. The rejection and the shame, it all became rocket fuel to prove myself to anyone and everyone in front of me.

That pain-driven motivation can be great to get you through the door, to break through the barriers standing in your way, but when the underlying issue is never addressed, you just continue to push down whatever was the root cause of your pain, deeper and deeper.

In high school after a messy few years and some lucky escapes from some real trouble, I finally decided to flip my life around. I lost over eighty pounds, switched friend groups from the bad kids to the jocks, cleaned my act up, and got my shit together. Finally dialling in on that future I so badly wanted. I built discipline and found structure in my life and went from barely scraping by to locking in on who I wanted to be and how I was going to get there.

Firefighting wasn't just a dream anymore; it became a mission. The golden ticket. The thing that would save me from myself.

And at twenty-one years of age, I made it. Fresh out of school, I got hired full-time. I turned my dream into reality.

It felt like everything I had worked for, every lonely night and every quiet ache in my chest, or rumble in my once fat-covered belly, had finally paid off. I had a purpose. I had a title. I had a tribe. A brotherhood. A family of heroes I could be a part of. I was one of them. I had a place to belong.

And for a while, it was everything.

The way people looked at me in uniform. Or the way kids waved at the trucks as we drove by. The nod from the old guy at the coffee shop who said, "Thank you for your service." The smiles from almost every passerby. The weight of the helmet, the gear, and the smell and smear of smoke and flames from fires past —it was everything I had dreamed of. It gave me hope. It gave me identity. It gave me purpose.

I still remember the rush from the tones going off, my heart pumping adrenaline through my veins, as I'd step onto the truck, engine roaring, locked in, smiling ear to ear, ready for whatever was to come. The first time I crawled through a burning building, feeling the heat all around me, the thick, dark smoke, crackling sounds from the fire burning, not even able to see my hand in front of my face, just listening and feeling my way through. Controlled chaos at its finest.

It scared the hell out of me. But it also felt like home—the only place I belonged. And I loved it. In the darkness, in the fire, I could risk it all, and I was doing something that mattered. *I* mattered. And I had finally found something more than myself that had meaning.

That in itself is beautiful, because sometimes the greatest meaning lives outside of ourselves. That's the heart of service: giving without needing anything in return.

The problem was, I wasn't just serving—I was stacking my worth on the validation it brought me. On how others saw me. On being the hero, a pillar in the community, collecting respect and appreciation as proof that I mattered, instead of first finding that worth inside of me.

When you're constantly yearning for others to fill your cup, you'll never be able to fill your own. What I'd been searching for was never actually out there. It was something that had to be found through looking at myself in the proverbial mirror and asking why.

So often, you chase something external, even a dream, thinking it will fix the cracks within us. Thinking that the right job, right title, and right love will finally hold us together. And then you finally get what you wanted, and something still aches; like feeling your heartbeat in your big toe after stubbing it.

Healing doesn't come from crossing some imaginary finish line. It starts the moment you stop hiding from whatever internal narrative you have looping inside your mind. From a limiting belief you once created to protect yourself that no longer serves you.

When we speak about forgiveness, it isn't about pretending these moments of rejection or pain didn't hurt but instead being able to let go of the story, that the pain you feel, or the limiting belief you hold, is all that you are. It's about deciding that the pain and the story that broke you doesn't have to define you anymore.

What I needed was a way back to myself. That meant freeing the deepest parts of me I'd been suppressing for so long.

It's easier to point the finger at everyone else—at every other issue. Easier to bury the truth, numb the pain, and keep pushing forward, head down, nose to the grindstone, than to face what's just beneath the surface.

I had to point that finger back at me. Not with blame, but with accountability, acceptance, and forgiveness.

But as we all know, that's much easier said than done. Throughout life, there are always turning points. Those moments that break us, and may even teach us, if we're willing to listen and learn. Here was one of mine.

One night at work, a call came through that changed me. I didn't know it at the time, but something in me shifted that night, something I wouldn't begin to understand until almost a full decade later when the anger built, the fear took over, and the running escalated, to a point where I was out of control.

A young girl was crushed between two semis. As strange as it sounds, it was just another call. Or at least, that's what I kept telling myself. I was riding the back of the engine that night when we pulled up under the overpass. Chaos was already unfolding—twisted metal, flashing lights, traffic backed up for miles. An SUV ripped to shreds, barely recognizable. The driver's seat crushed into the back of the car. One crew was already on-scene and more were pulling in behind us.

And there she was. Still in the seat, suspended, almost floating. And for a second, I thought I recognized her. Black hair. Nose piercings. It couldn't be. *But maybe?* I didn't say anything. I couldn't. I was still so young, new to the job, and all I knew was to keep my head down, do the work, and shut up.

The Jaws of Life did what they were supposed to. Wielding them like weapons, the guys peeled away metal and cut away the wreckage around her like paper—cutting through what they could. But it was too late. She was gone.

I still remember this single drop of blood, sliding down her cheek just like a tear, sitting there. A horrific and yet almost poetic image I'll never forget. It told the whole story without saying a word.

Another tragedy. And yet, just another Tuesday.

We covered at a different station overnight and didn't return to our own hall until the next morning. I hadn't had my phone with me, so I still didn't know if this girl was the one I knew. The one I'd grown up with. But I didn't say anything. That's not what you do. You're a man. Or at least, a boy pretending to be one.

When we got back to the hall, I went to grab my stuff. My bed was still made from the night before. Normally a no-go for a rookie, something you'd get at least a good earful for. But we hadn't even been at the hall, so I assumed it would be understandable. Still, a senior firefighter walked in and tore into me without hesitation, like I'd been fucking around on purpose. No pause. No question. Just ripping me apart.

Normally I'd laugh and move on. Part of the game, you fuck up, you take it.

But not like this.

I was mentally and emotionally at my limits. So, I snapped. After what I was holding in, I broke. I couldn't see straight. All I saw was red, and all I felt was betrayal.

And maybe he didn't know. How could he have? I hadn't said a word about what was going on inside. It's not what men do. But it didn't matter. Something in me cracked wide open that day and, looking back, it's what they would call a perfect storm for the onset of PTSD.

Experiencing a traumatic event, combined with a negative interaction surrounding it—whether that be shaming, blame, or even a joke at your expense—can result in PTSD. Now, this is something I didn't realize until over a decade later. But that moment, that specific day, was when something inside me truly fractured.

The armour I'd wrapped myself in for years began to fall apart, and that break leaked into everything that followed. That call cracked something open.

No one tells you what to do when you go home and the fire's out, when the gear is hung and the adrenaline fades, and you're left alone, standing in the dark, staring into nothing with that thousand-yard gaze that creeps in after a shift you can't talk about with anyone.

But wait a second.

This job gave me purpose. It gave me identity, belief, and something real to hold on to. I was a man. On paper, it should've been enough—the brotherhood, the title, the respect. I had everything I thought I needed. And yet, underneath it all, the weight was still there, waiting.

And that's what men do, right? We show up, we hold it in, we don't flinch, we laugh it off, we drink a little more, numb it out, and we keep. Moving. Forward.

Here's the real truth.

Often, it's only after a man is truly broken that he begins to find himself.

All of it continued to add up—the weight, the silence, the stories I kept telling myself about what strength looked like, what it meant to be a man, and who I thought I had to be in order to belong, to be enough. All of it lived inside the narratives I had created in my own mind.

Until it reached a point I couldn't ignore anymore.

All the weight I was carrying had started long before that one call and continued to get worse long after. Compounding, the pain began to bleed into all of it. The job, the relationships, the quiet moments—nothing was untouched.

A few years later whilst on a ski trip, a close friend of mine fell off a building while scaling the outside of it. We tried to resuscitate him, performing mouth to mouth and CPR. It was eleven days before his twenty-sixth birthday. He didn't make it.

Another crack.

A few months after that, my relationship with my long-term partner and fiancé ended.

Another crack.

More work. More drinking. More drugs. More sex. More

parties. More travel. More running. More blame. Anything to not face the truth.

It's pretty surreal how high functioning someone can be all the while holding on by a thread.

Just keep running and deflecting. If you just keep going, it'll never catch up to you.

Except that's not how it works.

And maybe that's where you see yourself.

Because this story isn't just about me. It's not just about firefighting.

This is about anyone who's spent years trying to hold it all together. Who's carried all their trials and tribulations and hid their wounds and scars—hid all their suffering quietly. For the ones who looked strong on the outside but felt lost on the inside.

Maybe you've had your own version of this story. A moment when your armour cracked. A relationship ending in heartbreak. A loved one or a friend dying. A betrayal that cut deeper than you could have ever imagined. A moment in which the world stopped, and you were never the same after.

For me, that breaking continued to show up. In the grief I didn't face. In the way I snapped at the people I loved. In the bottle I continued to reach for when I didn't want to feel. I'd hide so I could feel a version of living that didn't hurt. Just trying to find something, anything, that could quiet the storm inside.

That's what I knew how to do. And I continued to blame and point that finger at everyone else. I blamed the system, the department, the silence, the culture, and even the friends and loved ones that turned their backs on me. But the biggest blame lay somewhere else. It took me a long time to realize this, but at the heart of it all, I blamed myself. Under that blame was someone who didn't know how to ask for help. Someone who didn't think they were allowed to.

We all carry more than we let on, I get it. And if you're tired from running—emotionally, mentally, spiritually—it's not that you're weak. You're worn out. Burnt out. And tired of holding it all in.

Blame is a seductive lady of the night, because it makes us feel like we're always in the right.

But peace doesn't come from being right. It comes from choosing to take responsibility for what's going to happen next.

Forgiveness begins when you stop asking the past to fix itself and start deciding how you want to live your life from here on out.

Forgiveness gives us the power to live out our future, unchanged, unharmed from the external pain, because we've reclaimed our worth from the inside out.

So here it is: Yes, blaming is easier. It gives us somewhere to put the pain. Momentarily. A place holder. But it also keeps us stuck. It keeps us small. It keeps us at war with things we'll never be able to change.

Maybe you can relate. Maybe this hits home more than you'd like to admit. Blaming your partner, your parents, your boss, your ex, the systems, the world for all the ways your heart has been broken. And maybe some of that blame is valid. Some people do let us down. Some systems are broken. Some choices weren't fair. But blaming won't fix the past. And it doesn't change it, either. It just keeps you carrying the weight that isn't yours to hold anymore. And staying stuck in that loop robs you of something much more important: your own power.

Forgiveness isn't saying it didn't hurt. It's not saying it was okay. It's saying you're done letting it define you anymore.

When I was officially diagnosed with PTSD in September of 2023, I was still blaming. Still furious. Still waiting for support and an apology that was never going to come. But something in me started to shift.

I realized that the pain wasn't just about what happened. It was about what I had decided to keep holding on to, and the story I wasn't willing to let go of. The pain of being betrayed. The pain of not being seen. The pain of having no idea about what to do with everything I felt inside. And so, I had two options: let the pain take over my life or do the one thing I hadn't tried—stop blaming.

So, I stopped blaming, and I started facing it. Looking inward. Asking why. Slowly. Imperfectly. With two steps forward and one step back. Honestly. And I continue to point that finger back at myself, not to blame, but to take accountability for my future. For the chapters in my book that have not yet been written. For all that's still to come. It's not a linear journey, and truly feeling your emotions and facing them head on is, hands down, the hardest thing I've ever done.

But it's real. It works. And it's mine. And through it, I'm finally able to understand myself, my worth, and learn to truly respect and love every part of me. And as I struggle through that understanding, I've never felt more at home, more alive, and more in alignment with myself and my life.

Just like your journey is yours. Through all your own trials and tribulations, successes and failures (lessons), through your pain and your heartbreak, and all the moments that have broken you and filled your cup with joy—those are all yours, all a gift. Although many moments don't feel like lessons, when you assess those times in your life and see how they're actually opportunities you can choose to learn from, that propel you into your future of what you do or don't want, or what you will or won't allow in your life, you take your power back.

That's the lesson. Not just in my story, but in yours, too.

You're not weak for feeling. You're not wrong for hurting. But you don't have to carry that pain, that blame, that hurt forever. That's the difference. You get to let go. You get to forgive. You get to stop blaming. Not because *they* deserve peace, but for a reason so much more important—*you* deserve it.

So, stop letting the choices of others live inside your nervous system and run your day-to-day. Forgiveness is how you take your life back. You don't need to excuse the abuse, the betrayal, the neglect, but by letting it go, it means you stop building your identity around it. You stop carrying what isn't yours.

You create space for the good stuff to finally come in again. All the love, trust, peace, and joy that you deserve. And if that sounds impossible, start small. Breathe. Speak your truth. Ask why. Over and over again. Dive deeper. And remember you're alive; you have a life to live. Nothing is better than knowing that single fact. The fact that you're here today, reading this book, breathing—you made it. And you can do this. Take your power back. Let go. And forgive.

Adam Kunder is a resilience coach, keynote speaker, author, and former firefighter who spent over a decade on the frontlines before his own battle with PTSD, addiction, and loss brought him to his knees, and ultimately back to himself. He is the founder of Resilient Ones, a coaching program helping individuals rebuild their identity, reclaim their worth, and face what they've been running from. He believes healing doesn't begin when the pain stops. It begins the moment you stop running from it.

# THE SPACE BETWEEN APOLOGY AND FORGIVENESS IS GRACE

LYDIA KNORR

> To forgive is to set a prisoner free and discover the prisoner was you.
>
> Lewis B. Smedes

It's been more than a decade since the 3 a.m. phone call came in—the one that delivered the cruelest news imaginable. Without warning, I became a widow.

Nothing prepares you for the moment your life divides itself into before and after. The world keeps moving, even as you stand still, trying to understand how everything you knew could vanish in an instant.

Three days earlier when I was dropping Mike off at the airport for his business trip to China, my heart was so heavy saying goodbye because I could see the toll that the months of travels and time zones were having on him. As we pulled up to the terminal, I turned to him and said, "I'm worried about you.

You're aging before my eyes and I don't like what this business is doing to you." He looked at me with a weary smile I had become accustomed to, squeezed my hand and said, "I'll see you Sunday."

Three days later when he didn't come down for a morning meeting, his colleagues went to check on him and found him dead. The coroner's report came back inconclusive, citing a sudden arrhythmia for reasons unknown. Mike was just forty-nine years old, and a hero to us all—myself and our three daughters. How were we going to live without him?

Now, as the morning sun creeps across the kitchen counter, lighting up the quiet space where I sit with my second cup of coffee, I am alone, but not really. The weight of the past is beside me, unspoken, but present. Next to me is an unsent letter—words I've written and rewritten, yet still not feeling quite right.

There are things I want to say to my children. Some I've said before and some things I didn't know how to say—namely how to ask for their forgiveness. It's not to ease my conscience or erase what's been done. It's to unburden them. Because resentment and anger, like addiction, can be a weight too heavy to carry.

There were so many conversations we had had, ones I never imagined we would. They weren't loud or dramatic, just uncomfortably honest.

When my oldest daughter was in university, she rarely came home. She deliberately stayed away, and I know it was because she resented me for the way I coped after her dad died. One Sunday afternoon, I went to visit her. We decided to take a walk through the trails around her campus. At first, we didn't speak very much. We just walked along in silence. After some time, she broke the silence and told me she had been going to therapy for several months through a service offered by the university because she could no longer bear the weight of what she had pushed down for so many years. She told me that after her dad died when she was in high school, she felt she lost not only one parent, but two, because even when I was in the room, oftentimes I wasn't present for her or her sisters, and she didn't know how to talk to me anymore. She felt she needed to be the strong one in the family because I had fallen apart, absorbed in my own grief and unhealthy coping habits (drinking too much). My behaviour created an unsettling and unstable environment for them, so she stepped in, assuming the role of the adult in our home. In doing so, it forced her to bury her feelings of grief for almost four years after her dad died, until she finally hit a breaking point and sought help.

As I listened to her recount her experience and imagined what she must have felt (and buried), my heart ached for the instability my selfishness had created in my daughters' lives. I told her how sorry I was for placing that burden on her and when I asked what she needed from me now, she said, "Nothing"—a painful but honest response.

She explained that when she needed her mom, she didn't feel I was available, and now that she was grown and feeling more settled into herself, she didn't feel she needed anything from me at all.

Despite the warmth of the sun shining upon us, I had never felt a greater darkness in my heart and disgust in myself for this horrible situation I had created.

I knew that now was not the time to ask for her forgiveness. Now was the time to give her the space to feel seen, heard, and validated and to treat her as the adult she had become.

I thanked her for her honesty and told her that in whatever capacity she needed me to be—parent, peer, or otherwise—I would do everything possible to be present for her from this moment forward.

But the burden of being the responsible adult in our home wasn't hers to bear alone. While she was away at school, my middle daughter frequently took on the role of spokesperson after a night of my unhealthy coping. Each time, I would be given the same "talking to." I would be told how much my irresponsible behaviour upset her and her sisters, that they needed me to do better and be a better parent. And throughout the week, I was ... but come Friday and Saturday nights, I went down a rabbit hole, turning to wine as my companion.

Until one day when there was a conversation that hit differently. My daughter looked me straight in the eye and said, "You do know that if we didn't care, we wouldn't be having these conversations with you, right?" I nodded my understanding.

She continued, "But honestly, Mom, we've all talked about it, my sisters and me, and we're not sure how many more conversations we care enough to have."

And then there was silence.

With her eyes locked on mine, it took every fibre of my being not to get up and run away from that moment. I was so devastated by this painful truth from my daughter that I wanted to run away and pretend that none of this was happening.

I wanted to run away from myself.

The fact that my children had to sit *me* down, repeatedly, to give me a "talking to" was shameful. *I* was the parent—not them. And yet somehow, they had all, at some point or another, assumed the role of the adult in our home. When I realized that her words (and the words of my oldest daughter when she said she needed nothing from me) was their way of saying they had pretty much given up on me, it landed in a way that only the truth can—hard and clear. It was such a sobering moment.

What I wanted to say was, "I'm doing my best. The pain of losing your dad has hollowed me out and alcohol is my way of filling that emptiness." But I didn't, because this wasn't about me. It was about the impact my actions were having on my daughters.

So, I stayed quiet, and I listened. I really listened. I let her words and all the words they had shared with me over the years settle without interruption, and I tried to meet them with humility, not defensiveness.

That, I learned, is the difference between apology and forgiveness. *Apology speaks. Forgiveness listens.* And sometimes, the most powerful thing you can say is nothing at all.

It took years for me to get to a place of self-forgiveness and healing. There were nights when I'd sit on the edge of my bed, hands folded in prayer, and whisper apologies into the dark. I'd write "I forgive myself" in my journal, but that didn't make it true. What it did do, however, is open a door—one that led to compassion and helped me understand that forgiveness isn't saying that what I did was okay. It's saying that I will no longer define myself by my worst moments.

Now, so many years later, after having lived through the fire of my shame and sorrow, I have forgiven myself ... mostly. With some deep inner work and some outside help from therapy, I have come to understand myself more. I see myself changing, and I like what I am discovering. But I know this healing will be a lifelong practice—not a single event. Seeking my daughters' forgiveness is not for me. It's for them, because I don't want my children carrying the weight of what was never theirs to hold.

And somehow, beautifully, they have already laid that weight down. I see it in the grace they have shown me—how they still call to update me about everything that is happening in their lives; in the way they still include me in their plans and activities; in their insistence on keeping family traditions alive; and in their small acts of kindness that tell me they have made room for progress as well as the pain.

There was a heartwarming moment a number of years ago, after I decided to take a very long break from alcohol. About six months into that period, I was having dinner one evening with two of my daughters, while the third was living away from home. They came into the kitchen with a gift bag and said, "There's something we want to give you, but we all want to be here when you open it, so let's call our sister on FaceTime."

The gift was a beautiful pair of teardrop pearl earrings that were so elegant. But even better was the card they wrote to me. It read:

> Our family is a circle of strength and love; every crisis faced together makes the circle stronger. This last year has been a big growing period for all of us, some more than others. We want to recognize your efforts and how far you've come. We know that it's been many years of battling temptations, emotions, and trying to do what's right for us. We have watched you take the reins on this difficult course, and we are so proud to see you taking control of the things that once hindered you. We are all feeling the positive effects of your strength and want you to understand the comfort and stability it helps us to feel. However, our family's path continues to unfold, we will be by your side, as we know we are stronger with each other.

My daughters have supported me through it all—the good times and the hard times. They've shown me their forgiveness through the actions of their hearts, and not the reminder of the memories. It doesn't mean they have forgotten. It means they've chosen love anyway, again and again. Their words and actions show me that love, even when fractured, is rebuilt in thoughtful gestures like that.

Today, I live differently. I show up with presence. I speak with care. I don't ask my kids to trust me blindly—I earn it with consistency. I don't force healing—I create space for it.

Apologies are spoken once, but they are proven daily. Addressing my relationship with alcohol is only one piece. Living with integrity is the rest.

When my daughters call me to tell me about their day, I stop what I'm doing and listen. I am present in a way I wasn't in those early years after their dad died. When they have a problem, I don't try to solve it. I just give them space to feel seen, heard, and validated—and I always will.

I know that healing isn't a straight line. There are still hard days. There are still moments when the past whispers cruel reminders. But now, I respond with grace, with groundedness, and with a willingness to keep trying.

I keep coming back to that letter—the one I never sent but have read a hundred times.

If I could say one thing, it would be this: "I am sorry for the hurt I caused you and proud of the strength you have shown. You are not responsible for my healing. But if I can live in a way that lightens your load, that is what I will do, every day." And that is the most honest form of grace I can offer.

Still, I needed to know how they truly felt. I finally found the courage to ask each of them if they could forgive the hurt I caused. Their answers brought both tenderness and truth—and the knowing I'd been waiting for.

Lydia Knorr is an award-winning speaker and author who inspires and transforms audiences to find grace, meaning, and resilience through life's hardest seasons.

# OH HENRY!

DR. I. MICHAEL KAUFMANN

> A good story goes beyond what a forgiving God cares to do: it reconciles families and unburdens them of secrets whose bond is stronger than blood. But in their revealing, as in their keeping, secrets can tear a family apart.
>
> ABRAHAM VERGHESE

Shame was my answer. I felt ashamed. The question posed by an audience member: "Why didn't you buy all those chocolate bars at one store, rather than going from one to the next?"

I was seated in a wing-chair on the stage of our village town hall, the place I called Morwick in my recently published book entitled *Drugs, Lies & Docs*, gazing at a hundred or so people, most of whom I knew from one walk of my life or another. Kat, my interlocutor, a lawyer, and a former family practice patient of mine when she was a child, was seated to my right, mic in hand, grinning Cheshire Cat-style. Between us was a low round table, a copy of my book we were launching displayed upon it. She had prepped me on the interview questions, but not that one.

Back then, I had lied to the folks at the cash. By my actions, I lied even when the truth was harmless. I was used to lying. There was so much I needed to keep secret. In the early days and months after I stopped using opioids and drinking, I craved sweets. I couldn't stop eating those Oh Henry! bars, so I wanted them to think they were an afterthought—that I really needed the toothpaste and the deodorant I brought to the counter; that the candy was an impulse buy. Same at the next store. And the next. The personal hygiene products were piling up in my bathroom cabinet. The Oh Henry!s disappeared immediately. This was but one thing I didn't want people in those pharmacies to know about me. Now, everything had changed; I wasn't about to lie to the assembled in the Morwick town hall.

By the time I had graduated from medical school and completed my residency in family practice, the seeds of my opioid dependence were deeply sown. I didn't grow up as a drug-abuser despite high school life in the booze-sodden psychedelic sixties. I tried cannabis once; I didn't like it. Sure, we drank some, as kids would do in those days, perhaps a bit more once released into the wilds of university life away from home. But frankly, I preferred tea, enjoyed with my girlfriend—who I liked a lot—served every afternoon after school by her mom, a practice never a part of my family tradition. I was aware, though, that my grandmother was an alcoholic and her daughter, my mother, loved her narcotic-containing migraine pills (and would later become addicted to opioids like me), but I never considered that family history meant I was at risk.

I was once asked when my opioid addiction began. There is no single point in time when the switch is flipped in the brain and a chronic disease appears where none existed moments before. But one incident does stand out.

As a medical student working an elective at a crazy-busy hospital in a Toronto suburb, I was on duty overnight, expected to run electrocardiograms (EKGs) for patients in the emergency room when required. "We need you, Mike," they said. "Right now," they said, yanking me from precious sleep in a strange and comfortless room. To add to that, I had a terrible cough left over from a summer cold that was also roused when the phone rang. My head ached with fatigue and my chest burned as I hacked my way into the ER. "Drink this," the nurse said, handing me a little cup of red syrup like Alice's Wonderland potion. I did, no question asked.

Before I finished running that EKG—the patient, clammy-cool and sweating, hauling breath through an oxygen mask—the magic arrived. For me, not him. The clenching muscles in my neck released, the barking was quelled, and my fatigue dissipated. Sure, I learned how to run EKGs and much more that summer, but the lesson that topped them all was that hydrocodone, the active ingredient in that cough medicine they gave me, melted my discomfort. *All of it.*

After that, like tossing a glowing cigarette butt into a barn filled with old straw, my opioid addiction caught fire, smouldering for a few more years while I finished my training, then erupting, unrestrained, only a handful of years into my life as a family doctor in Morwick, the rural Ontario town where I now sat.

Then, as now, they really needed family doctors in small towns like ours. I saw patients in my office every weekday. I delivered babies and worked ER shifts too many nights. I attended my hospital inpatients faithfully, around the clock every day of the week, never sharing on-call duties with colleagues I believed to be less well-trained than me, a tragic and misguided hubris. Nursing home visits, house calls, ambulance transfers—I did them all. I worked in the infirmary of the Morwick Correctional Institute, the local federal prison, seething with inmates wanting me to authorize dietary changes, fans for their cells, and lots more for which my medical training was irrelevant.

Two years of family practice residency training weren't enough for me—not for anyone, in my opinion—situated in a rural hospital setting with minimal back-up. The first day I stepped into the Morwick hospital ER there was a patient pulled down from a hydro pole, his tether snagged by a passing car. We did our best to stabilize his multiple traumatic injuries and rush him to another hospital where surgeons tried to save him. He died. If we had had a surgeon on staff at our hospital, would he have survived? Who knows, but in those days, there was no such help readily available.

Heart attacks, strokes, kids with severe asthma, women losing pregnancies, psychotic breaks, suicide attempts, drug overdoses, anything and everything. Just because we were perched in a bucolic, agricultural corner of the province didn't mean the human calamities were attenuated. In fact, the machinery the farmers used was particularly lethal.

One time, years into my tenure in Morwick, a young man was brought into the ER who had been pulled into a giant hay auger and spat out the other side into the wagon. He lay on his stomach on the gurney, huge blade gashes on his back, his legs stripped of flesh and muscle, feet ripped right off. "Is that you, Mike?" I heard him say. He recognized my voice. He survived that day only to be taken by a drug overdose after a few years sitting legless in front of our village pharmacy, chatting to passersby, looking for handouts. The image of those denuded legs, like chicken bones, still calcified in my memory, un-deletable.

"What was it like, using drugs while working, while seeing patients?" Wouldn't you know it: the very first question from a lady sitting at the edge of the front row would be the toughest.

The old town hall meeting room smelled musty when I was there earlier to scope it out, before all the folding chairs were positioned on either side of tables that ran the length of the room. Copies of my book were everywhere—more than I'd ever seen in one place before. Coloured light streamed in through the panes of stained glass above a small gallery across from the stage above the main entrance. I noticed the stale aroma was gone, cleansed by fresh air or maybe covered by the various scents dragged in by all the people.

There was a time when the answer to her question would have been likewise smothered by secrecy, twisted rationalization, and denial. But not now.

"The drugs helped me at first," I answered, "but that didn't last."

I started out as an opportunistic drug user. If a patient returned unused tablets, especially opioid pain medication, I accepted them as if they were a personal gift, and one to which I felt entitled. Ten or twelve pills would last a couple of days, longer if I wasn't working in the ER at night or up delivering a baby. They helped me relax, cope with the stress of work, focus, and function. They helped me stay awake when I needed that. Ironically, I used them to fend off the irritation of drug-seeking inmates at the prison, the Percocet tablets that made my day bearable palpable in my left front pocket.

Soon, rather than wait for random drug appearances in my office from patients or samples provided by the pharmaceutical representatives, I began skimming the opioid drugs I prescribed to palliative care patients I tended in their homes. How? By delivering the medications dispensed by the pharmacy myself as part of my home visits. No one ever noticed. Everyone trusted me.

I believed I was functioning at a high level, even including the night I admitted a patient from the ER with gastroenteritis and dehydration without seeing them in person as I should have done. Even when, the next day, I refused to sign that patient's order sheet because I didn't remember seeing them! True, I had been on duty the previous night, but I had taken sedatives and who knows what else to allow me some sleep. I had attended the patient remotely during what must have been a drug-induced blackout. The treatment was correct and appropriate, and the patient did well, but I was shaken.

Still, I didn't stop using drugs. In fact, when the tablets and cough preparations weren't showing up in my office sufficiently often to satisfy my growing need for them—especially as the pain and craving of withdrawal emerged—I began to inject small amounts of Demerol, an opioid commonly used for pain in those days. The first time, just a few milligrams under the skin, and wow! Not just relief from withdrawal, but deep, soothing euphoria. Later, I injected larger doses into the muscles of my arm or butt. Finally, I mainlined directly into my veins, leaving the injection scars—"track marks" like heroin addicts wear—all over my arms.

Once I'd experienced the "feel of steel," as the hardened drug users call self-injection with needle and syringe, there was no going back. I obtained the Demerol from the very pharmacy where I bought those Oh Henry! bars. "For office use," the prescriptions read, always filled without question because they trusted me. Well, I suppose in a perverse way that was true; I mostly injected myself when I was alone—in my office. But inexorably, as the flames become more intense, I'd shoot up in the office bathroom, even while attending to patients.

I also scored Demerol from the hospital. When I prescribed it for a patient in the ER, which was often—and too often, extra doses not really required—I would draw up the drug myself (relieving a nurse of that task) and swap the syringe for another I had pre-filled with saline, or something else, and hidden in my white coat. Some for them, some for me. On the wards, much the same.

Here is what happened when I injected Demerol into a vein: First, I felt the wallop of pleasure in my chest and the back of my throat. Then, the pain of withdrawal—or of anything, for that matter—melted. My tongue became thick and sticky, and I had to work to form my words. Sometimes those words drifted into gibberish until I pulled them back into line. My handwriting did the same, the ends of sentences on a patient record or hospital order sheet drifting into squiggles without meaning. The day after most ER shifts, I returned to the hospital and reviewed my records to see if they were sensible and legible. The effort to be present for a patient, to fend off the opioid dream state, exceeded that of formulating their problems. I don't remember the mistakes I might have made, but I do remember the faces of patients puzzled, or even upset, about something my garbled brain had just uttered.

Was anyone hurt? I don't know for sure. But I do know that these people who had entrusted me with their wellbeing didn't receive my best. I tried to stop using the drugs again and again, but my efforts always failed. There were times when colleagues—nurses and doctors—approached me. They cared about me, knew I was troubled, knew I needed help. I brushed them aside. I was sure that owning up would result in the loss of my medical license, my reputation, my very identity. And yet, my shame and isolation were so intense that there were days I thought dying would be my only way out and the best for all concerned.

My nightmare ended in the spring of 1986 on the day I met a colleague in the doctors' parking area behind the hospital. A chance encounter—or so I thought at the time. He pulled a scrap of paper from his pocket with a phone number scrawled on it.

Why did he have that on him? It was the number of the DOC helpline, and I was to call it right away. DOC stood for "Doctors On Chemicals." I thought that a stupid name, even if a catchy acronym—and an accurate description of me. He told me he would report me to the medical regulatory authorities if I didn't call; I feared that more than using to death. How perverse is that!

I left the hospital without going in and drove to my clinic, which was closed for the day. There, I sat at my desk positioned in the front of my office in a bay window facing the street, the curtains drawn. I stared at the phone. Should I call? I did what any addicted person would do: I injected myself with courage one last time. Then I called.

I was referred to a doctor who practiced addiction medicine and specialized in helping healthcare professionals who had substance use disorders. I didn't know any of those even existed. Then, it was on to residential treatment, whether I liked the idea or not. I never told anyone there about using drugs while seeing patients; that was my secret and one that separated me from all the other patients, rendered my transgressions more heinous than any of theirs; it kept me apart. I was disgusted with myself. How could someone like me, a professional who ought to know better, find themselves in an addiction treatment centre with all these others? How could I have done the things I did?

Before I was discharged, I joined a therapy group for healthcare professionals addicted to drugs and alcohol—one that I would attend for years, but still, I didn't confess to practicing impaired. Afterwards, gradually returning to work and life in recovery, I stopped thinking about what had happened, preferring, instead, the notion that my medical skills were so well honed and my competence so unconscious that I hadn't harmed anyone.

That belief carried me through another decade of family practice and on to my new career as founding Medical Director of the Physician Health Program of the Ontario Medical Association. This was the service that replaced the old DOC program—the very one I had called—now defunct. There, we developed policies and procedures designed to prevent doctors from working while impaired, to support our Hippocratic Oath of first doing no harm. That old idea that we could get away with it, that we could function adequately well while in the face of evolving substance use disorders, could no longer sit well with me. Recovery encourages self-awareness and evaluation, resolution of resentments, making amends wherever possible, forgiveness for others, and even for ourselves. I learned to live with my faults, correct those I could, and play to my strengths. I stopped using drugs and alcohol. I slept well most of the time.

Eventually, though, the grain of sand in your shoe that you barely noticed becomes a tiny pebble, then a larger one, then a jagged stone. You can ignore its presence for only so long. But unlacing the shoe and dumping it isn't so easy. I needed help. First, I told Father Joe, my recovery sponsor, about my secret and persistent feelings of guilt when I listed my resentments and transgressions, as we were encouraged to do. He understood and did not judge me. I guess that was a bit like confession in the Catholic sense, but I had no tradition of any of that, and this certainly wasn't anything religious, even if I was talking to a priest sitting in a rectory!

After that, I would mention my guilt feelings in recovery meetings and, again, folks nodded and accepted what I shared. Much later, at a recovery meeting as part of a convention for recovering doctors (yes ... there is such a thing!), the keynote speaker read a poem called "Shameless," which was about self-love and forgiveness. The message really spoke to me: Remove the mask of shame, accept ourselves as perfect works-in-progress, pour rapturous praise all over ourselves, we have it all, we have it all! These things helped a lot, but the people I cared about so much—my former patients—I couldn't speak to directly; they couldn't nod and accept. There was still a pebble stuck in my shoe.

About halfway through the book launch event, there was a short break. There were some snacks spread out on a table at the back of the hall, and I made my way there. I saw an elderly couple angling towards me. He was stoney faced and she looked nervous. They looked familiar, but I wasn't sure how I knew them. Before I could grab a snack, the lady approached and asked if she and her husband could talk to me for a moment. It was important.

"We were your patients," she said. "This one time when I had an appointment with you, you fell asleep right in front of me. I didn't think that was right, but I didn't know what to do."

Her husband watched us, grim. She looked like she might cry. I felt the same way. Then, she hugged me.

"I'm so glad you're okay," she added.

*That wasn't sleep*, I thought, knowing a narcotic nodding off was much more likely. I must have injected myself just prior to that interview. Oh, geez ...

I thanked her, told her how much her message meant to me, and made my way back to the stage. Kat asked me some more questions and invited still more from the audience. I answered them on autopilot in the hazy aftermath of my encounter with my former patient, as though nothing else mattered any longer.

The hands on a clock poised high on the wall across from me read 7:50, unhelpful because it was the same time it had displayed two hours earlier when we arrived. Yet, I knew we had gone overtime. A woman rose to ask one last question. She was young, too young to have been around in the days when I was a troubled family doctor in the community. She commanded my attention by asking the question I had been waiting for, hoping for: "Why did you write this book?"

I rhymed off the usual things: the preservation of my teaching about addiction to medical students; how I wanted to champion the concept of Recovery as I knew it; an offering of hope to those who suffered addiction and their families. I stopped momentarily as I worked up to my usual closing—how writing was a healing journey for me. But I didn't mention that. Instead, I finished this way: "I wrote this book for you ... to say I'm sorry for what happened." I paused, leaving those words suspended in mid-air. Did I really say that out loud? The very thing I had long dreamed of saying to former patients but dared not for fear of upsetting them? As I looked out at so many familiar faces, I added, "But I think things turned out pretty well."

I heard applause. Then "thank yous" all around. There were some hugs. I felt light and wanted to float about the room like a honeybee, flower to flower, but there was a table set for me at the front of the room to sign books and a line was already forming. Before I could reach it, a man pushed forward. I didn't recognize him, and he didn't introduce himself. He didn't ask me to sign a book. He said he had something for me, that he had thought about giving me some toothpaste and maybe some deodorant, but no.

"This would be perfect," he said.

It was an Oh Henry! bar.

Dr. I. Michael Kaufmann is a retired family and addiction medicine physician and the founding Medical Director of the Physician Health Program, a service in support of doctors in Ontario who need help with substance use and other mental health problems. He is proudly an opioid addict in Recovery, a music lover and maker, and husband to wife Judy of fifty years.

# THE TENTH GOODBYE

MELANIE GOLDMAN

When you live with a diagnosis of borderline personality disorder (BPD), most individuals have had to hear the word "forgiveness" more times than they can count. Most of my life, I held on to anger and resentment because that's what living in survival is. It kept me safe, but it also kept me extremely small. Because when you finally have to cut the cord or accept when things are over, what does it mean then? The word "over"—as in "done"—that all used to really terrify me, and to be honest, it still does, especially with the diagnosis and trauma. It reminds me of slammed doors and rejection, of grief, of chasing people who never really loved me back, of waiting for texts that never came, and of dreams that never came true. But then this final break, this last goodbye, showed me it wasn't them I was chasing—it was always me.

In the heartbreaking silence this last year of being truly alone, there's nothing that can shatter your entire life and cut through all the truth you never wanted to face. But when you're alone, heartbroken in your own silence, there is only truth, and it's *loud.* My truth was: I never loved myself enough. And I never knew how.

I feel that as humans, we don't know how to thank our pain. We hate it. We blame it. But my ugly ass pain is the only reason I can finally breathe. I have lived so long in survival mode that it has become the only normal I know. But when you finally begin to breathe, you realize you can't breathe the old air anymore.

As painful as it was being in that friendship—and all the relationships I once clung to—cutting them off was hard, but it was the only way I could actually start to learn how to love myself moving forward.

The hardest part of healing that people don't discuss is the loneliness that comes from letting go of everything and everyone and learning to trust the world again as it still feels shaky below you. Explaining every shedding layer of pain to people is exhausting, and going away can be triggering in itself. You see, this wasn't the first time that I had gone through this type of situation—where I was trying to excuse my way back into the same situation over and over again. So this time I wasn't going to run back and say I was sorry because I had just ghosted, or sorry because I had disappeared to heal. I tried over and over to control situations, to say I was sorry, to try to minimize, to figure it out. But there was nothing to figure out except how to learn to love myself through this.

In every lonely night, in every lost amount of sleep, I needed to learn that I wasn't going to love myself in a relationship that was breaking. I needed to learn to love myself while I was breaking. And to be honest, I kept crying out, and slowly through every crack I realized I needed to learn to love my cracks. Because it's in the imperfection, it's in the fear, and it's in sitting in it that we start to love again. I realized that God didn't want me to run from any of it. He wanted me to love all of it, and to surrender, to have humility, that comes with a whole lot of people who don't always understand your healing.

My husband once said, "Who cares if they don't understand you? Why are you trying so hard to get people to understand you when life is about being in your own silly little world and allowing people to understand that? If you let people into your world, those are the people that are supposed to stay."

I kept trying to fit my life and my way into other people's worlds instead of realizing that healing is lonely—that life can be lonely—and people can come into my world if they would like to. So instead of trying to explain every shedding layer of my pain to people who never really understood it—or weren't ready to hear it —I realized none of that mattered anymore. It was about me not making myself small—physically or emotionally. It was not about me comparing, contrasting, fighting, or competing. It was about me getting out of that type of race and me just living the race of being. And when you get out of that battle, you watch other people around you start to scramble. And it's not a mean thing to say, but I feel like most of us are on this treadmill, and we're not going to get out alive anyway. *So, what are we all fighting each other for?*

I started to realize that a lot of the relationships I had around me were with people that didn't make my nervous system feel safe and didn't allow me to forgive the inner child within me that never felt settled. They weren't really relationships at all. They were more like competitors I was in this big arena with, fighting a big battle with me.

And so, instead of doing that anymore, I put my sword up and I said, "I don't want to do this anymore." Because I've lived in fight-or-flight since I was a child—addicted to proving, and defending, and waiting for this approval, but it never came. So not getting the apology was actually the biggest blessing I've ever felt. An apology always felt like a war, like a daily fight for my life. But I didn't want to live in war anymore, and I couldn't carry any more post-traumatic stress disorder (PTSD). So, for all intents and purposes, I was hanging up my competitive coat.

I decided to forgive myself because I could not handle it anymore. And my goodbye, for me, was about welcoming all the emotions and letting life just be.

## The Moment It All Broke

I still remember the day the person I once called my best friend—my sister—said, "Maybe you don't want this relationship in your life." What I heard was that *she* didn't want the relationship anymore.

It was the tenth time she had pushed me away and the tenth time I came back, believing that this time she'd finally choose me the way I chose her.

We were supposed to be inseparable. I had dreamed of living next door to her, helping raise children together with our husbands, sharing holidays and secrets like sisters do. But that day, the words hit me like a punch to the chest. I was sitting in my living room, the sunlight slipping through the blinds, but it felt darker than I'd known.

I wanted to cry out, to beg her to stay. Instead, I sat there, numb. Instead of me trying to plead and go back and forth, I went silent. I went dead inside. I went completely dead inside for months. And then something in me just blocked her. Whether that was right or wrong, I just didn't know what else to do anymore. Part of me knew that the cycle needed to end. The cycle had to end long before that.

It wasn't real, and as much as I was trying to make it real, it just wasn't. It was another illusion I was trying to make real in my life. I had spoken deeply about this relationship with God, to other practitioners, mentors, gone to Sedona, and so many times with my husband watching me suffer about this relationship, saying he was so uncomfortable—about why this even felt like more than a relationship to me strangling my energy alive. I tried to justify it over and over again—*oh no, it's fine, we're best friends.*

It wasn't even just that statement, it was so many times that I had pushed my life away for other people. I had felt awful for years, yet why wasn't I saying goodbye?

I realized it wasn't about this person—it was about love in general. To truly forgive myself, and to truly love myself, I knew what I needed to do. I knew I wasn't going to get anything from going through the same cycles over and over again. I wanted to write so many things throughout the months. I wanted to say so many things. But what I truly wanted to say was: "I love you so much, but I can't do this anymore. It's killing me, and you know this too." And the truth is, the goodbye was already there a long time before it ended.

## The Illusion of Forever

When we first met, I thought I had found a soulmate. Hours of voice notes, laughter, nicknames, dreams. She was family to me—a rare, bright light in a cold world. Everything about us mirrored each other: our childhood wounds, our paths in music, even our husbands. The symmetry felt divine. Our energy was electric. For someone like me, that was everything.

But slowly, cracks showed: messages unanswered, subtle distance. She started disagreeing with my dreams, telling me she didn't see them the way I did. Each dismissal was a fracture. I told myself, "She's going through a lot. It's just me. I'll just love more."

This was the same old story—shrinking to be accepted, dimming my light to belong. I had done it since I was a child in a chaotic house. And here I was again, silencing my truth to keep someone else close. Except I was wrong. This was not real love.

## The Pattern

Looking back now, I see this wasn't the first time. It was just the latest chapter in a long history of loving too much and being left behind. Friends, lovers, even family members—I'd chased their affection like a child chasing fireflies, desperate to catch just one. I wanted to be enough.

I held on to the fantasy that if I loved hard enough, if I showed up again and again, they would stay. But the truth was, I was building a castle on sand.

When I was young, I learned that being loved meant hiding parts of myself—making myself smaller so others wouldn't feel overwhelmed.

*Am I too much?*

*Am I not enough?*

*What's wrong with me?*

These questions echoed in the quiet moments, as I lay awake wondering why no one seemed to want the whole me.

## Sedona: The Reckoning and the Call to Forgive Myself

I decided to take a trip to Sedona, and something shifted two weeks into the spiritual retreat. During a session with a practitioner, while doing inner child work, I felt like I connected with my higher self. I started asking God, "What's wrong with me?"

I heard a response: "Nothing's wrong with you, but you need to radically accept people for exactly who they are. You have to stop trying to do my job."

I also kept hearing, "You're not selfish for wanting more. You're not selfish for needing more—for needing reciprocity. You're not selfish for needing truth. But most of all, you're not selfish for needing love, and you're not selfish for needing to love yourself."

I had been chasing the love I never gave myself—from my childhood, to my music career, to my diagnosis. I kept trying to prove I was enough to people who felt just as lost inside themselves. They were drawn to my energy.

I wasn't too little. I wasn't too much. I wasn't unworthy. But I had spent my life around people who knew how to drain my energy—who recognized the light in me. So when my friend said those words—"Maybe you don't want this relationship in your life"—I realized, despite the pain, I needed to hear them more than anything.

Those words ripped me open—not just in that moment, but across decades of rejection. Every summer at camp where I felt overweight and alone. Every boyfriend who walked away. Every time I sat packed and ready, waiting, and no one came. It wasn't just her goodbye. It was every goodbye I had ever swallowed.

And in Sedona, I finally began to grieve—the girl I never became, the love that never came, all the times I believed I wasn't enough. And through that grief, I started to forgive myself.

## The Hardest Forgiveness

I kept thinking I needed to forgive her. For lying. For failing me. But that wasn't the real forgiveness.

Forgiveness came in pieces, like shards of glass. Just when you think you've gathered them, another cut appears. I see it with my clients, too—people thinking they've forgiven, but the pain still plays on repeat. Some days were easier than others. Just when you think you've gone through all the dark shadows, here comes another one. Because real forgiveness isn't about the other person. It's about all the ugly truth within yourself: your ownership, your courage, your surrender.

I had to let it die in a thousand deaths, alone in a thousand stories I had on repeat. I still have to admit it in a thousand hurt moments of shouting alone. But one day, you wake up and you realize: *Wow. How did I get here? And why did I let myself get here?*

Forgiveness is in the anger at yourself, in the anger at the world. I was the one I had abandoned. I abandoned myself. I was angry at myself. Forgiveness is in every stage of grief. And forgiveness is not easy.

One night, when the loneliness felt unbearable, I found myself talking quietly to the younger version of me—the little girl who kept hoping, kept believing, kept waiting.

I said, "Hey, it's okay. I see you. I see how hard you keep trying to be enough, how much you want to be loved for exactly who you are. But honestly, everyone is struggling. Every single person on this planet is carrying their own pain. Until you realize that, until you truly understand that you don't need anyone but yourself, you'll always be searching outside for that love."

In that moment, we took a full breath together—a deep inhale that filled our souls. As we embraced, I reminded her, "You're not too little. You're not too much. You're simply you, just the way God made you, and that's perfectly okay."

I told her, "It's okay to be scared. It's okay to be alone, because God is with you, and so is everyone else, even when it doesn't feel that way. Everyone feels this way."

And in that quiet space, we chose to let go of waiting—waiting for anyone else to save us or love us fully. Because the truth is, *you are worthy* of taking that step forward, right now, for yourself. Forgiving myself for staying too long was the beginning of coming home to who I truly am.

## The Unbecoming and Becoming

After that day, things started to change. I stopped reaching out to people who didn't reach back. I began setting boundaries where I had none. I allowed myself to rest. To cry. To say no. I had never said no before.

It wasn't easy. It was super lonely. Some nights, the old questions crept back in. But slowly, I started to stand taller in my own skin. I found my holy angels.

I was finally choosing me.

The absence of those old relationships stopped screaming. It started whispering truths I couldn't hear before.

## A Quiet Freedom

Forgiveness isn't a clean cut. It's a scar that reminds me I survived loving too hard and still came home to myself.

Maybe forgiveness isn't about perfection or forgetting. Maybe it's simply a quiet whisper in the mirror saying, "I forgive you for waiting. For hoping. For loving them more than they could hold. And I choose you now."

Forgiveness isn't about erasing the hurt. It's about admitting, honestly, that something still hurts. My heart still breaks, but now I know if I hadn't gone through all of this, I couldn't forgive myself. I couldn't love myself. I couldn't help my clients. I couldn't help myself.

And to be honest, even if I feel heartbroken, I also feel my heart more than I ever have before. And so, I wouldn't ever take anything away in my life, because I love people more than I ever have now. I know more things than I ever have now. And my scars are a reminder that I'm the greatest version of myself now.

And to anybody else who feels a deep pain so far in their chest that they can't see a way of forgiving another person, just remember: it's never about them. It's always about *you.*

Melanie Goldman is a Registered Psychotherapist with a Master of Arts in Counselling Psychology and a dedicated advocate for those living with borderline personality disorder (BPD). For more than a decade, she has worked in the mental health sector as a speaker, writer, peer facilitator, and educator, raising awareness and challenging stigma across Canada. Trained in dialectical behavioural therapy (DBT) and cognitive behavioural therapy (CBT), she is passionate about helping others find hope and healing. BPD and bipolar disorder have touched her own family, and she continues to help others discover their own "Rae of Light in the Darkness."

## Life to Paper Publishing

An independent hybrid publishing house dedicated to helping individuals transform their life stories into meaningful books that foster connection, reflection, and positive change.

We specialize in memoir, personal narrative, and knowledge-based nonfiction, guiding authors through every stage of the publishing journey—from idea to manuscript to a professionally published book. Our approach is collaborative, thoughtful, and every book we publish supports our mission:

*To write a better future.*

Whether you are writing for personal legacy, community, or a wider audience, Life to Paper exists to support you in bringing your story to life.

**Learn more or begin your publishing journey:**

www.lifetopaper.com | @lifetopaper

## Life to Paper Foundation

A nonprofit organization dedicated to helping individuals impacted by mental health challenges and addiction experience the therapeutic power of storytelling.

Through writing programs, community initiatives, and access to publishing resources, we create opportunities for individuals to process their experiences, share their stories, and find connection through expression.

All proceeds from *When We Forgive* directly support this work.

**Learn more or support:**

www.lifetopaper.org | @lifetopaper_foundation

www.ingramcontent.com/pod-product-compliance
Lightning Source LLC
Chambersburg PA
CBHW031346230926
51848CB00002B/405
* 9 7 8 1 9 9 7 9 2 9 0 2 4 *